BALANCING WATER

Before restoration,
Marsh Island Ranch,
California.

After restoration,
Marsh Island Ranch,
California.

Great Basin Canada geese
over Mount Shasta,
California.

Fall migration,

White Lake,

California.

BALANCING

RESTORING THE KLAMATH BASIN

WATER

Photographs by **TUPPER ANSEL BLAKE**

and **MADELEINE GRAHAM BLAKE**

Text by **WILLIAM KITTREDGE**

With quotations by Aldo Leopold

UNIVERSITY OF CALIFORNIA PRESS   BERKELEY   LOS ANGELES   LONDON

University of California Press
Berkeley and Los Angeles, California

University of California Press, Ltd.
London, England

Photographs © 2000 Tupper Ansel Blake and
Madeleine Graham Blake
Text © 2000 William Kittredge

The quotations displayed on pages 4, 17, 31, 33, 38, 43,
55, 93, 99, 102, 120, 128, 132, 136, 157, 160, and 163 are
drawn from Aldo Leopold's *A Sand County Almanac* and other
writings. They are used by kind permission of Nina Leopold
Bradley and the Shack Foundation.

Library of Congress Cataloging-in-Publication Data

Blake, Tupper Ansel.
    Balancing water : restoring the Klamath Basin /
photographs by Tupper Ansel Blake and Madeleine Graham
Blake ; text by William Kittredge.
        p.   cm.
    Includes index.
    ISBN 0-520-21314-9 (cl. : alk. paper).
    1. Water use—Klamath River Watershed (Or. and Calif.)
2. Klamath River Watershed (Or. and Calif.)   I. Title.
II. Blake, Madeleine Graham, 1948– .   III. Kittredge,
William.

GB991.K63 B63 2000
333.91'009795 21—dc21   99-044878

Printed and bound in Hong Kong

09   08   07   06   05   04   03   02   01   00
10   9   8   7   6   5   4   3   2   1

CONTENTS

ACKNOWLEDGMENTS

Ducks, geese, shorebirds, and cranes were working their way south. I had seen small, isolated groups in the Cariboo Parklands of British Columbia. A few weeks later in the Flathead River Valley of Montana I came upon wetlands that held a greater number of birds. Later, as I headed down the Snake River of Idaho and out across the desert of eastern Oregon, the horizon always held skeins of geese or flocks of ducks. Unknown to me, these birds and I were headed to the same place.

After dark on a cool, crisp November evening I reached my destination. Awakening at dawn, I was not prepared for what I was to witness. It was as if every waterfowl in western North America was either flying, swimming, loafing, or feeding in front of my eyes. It was fall and I was in the Klamath Basin, which straddles the Oregon-California border.

Later that day, as the sun was setting, I was photographing this wildlife spectacle, when a truck stopped. A man came up, introduced himself as Bob Fields, the manager of the Klamath Basin National Wildlife Refuge Complex. We talked wildlife, the wonder of the migration, and photography. We became friends. That was twenty-seven years ago.

Several years later, when I was collaborating with Starker Leopold on our book *Wild California,* I mentioned to him my experience in the Klamath Basin. Starker smiled, then spoke knowingly and glowingly of the region—its teeming wildlife, huge marshes, blue-ribbon trout streams and great expanses of forests and large ranches extending eastward from the snow-capped Cascade Range out into the Great Basin. Throughout his career as a professor of forestry and wildlife at the University of California he spoke out to preserve ALL the aforementioned whenever the opportunity arose.

Starker is now gone but the Klamath Basin is not. The Leopold influence still permeates the air. For you see, the folks of the Klamath Basin are in the midst of working out their future as a community, with water being both the catalyst and the tie that binds. To be successful in their quest, they must look at and protect ALL the components that make up their watershed. They are enacting what Starker's father, Aldo Leopold, called "the land ethic" in his classic memoir, *A Sand County Almanac.*

The land ethic that was conceived as theory is now being put into practice by the people of the Klamath Basin. I'd like to acknowledge them for doing so. I also want to thank two of Aldo's children, Nina and Luna, for their permission to use their father's quotes throughout our book. It is a fitting tribute to Aldo Leopold and his *Sand County Almanac,* on this the fiftieth anniversary of its publication.

This project succeeded because of the generosity and enthusiasm of a great many folks. I wish to thank Steve McCormick of the Nature Conservancy of California; Russ Hoeflich of the Nature Conservancy of Oregon; Glenn Olson and Dan Beard of the National Audubon Society; Karl Wirkus, U.S. Bureau of Reclamation; Douglas P. Wheeler; Secretary for Resources of California; Robert Fields, U.S. Fish and Wildlife Service (retired); Greg Thomas, Natural Heritage Institute; Jim Cole, Intermountain West Joint Venture; Leighton Taylor, Rusty Hale, and Jeanne Sedgwick, Packard Foundation; Dave Livermore of the Nature Conservancy of Utah; and Alice Kilham and Jim Carpenter, cochairs, the Hatfield Upper Klamath Basin Working Group.

Financial assistance came from individuals, corporations, foundations, government agencies, and conservation organizations. I greatly appreciate the trust and faith of the following project donors, whose support enabled the photographic survey to be undertaken and this book to be published.

Government agencies

U.S. Fish and Wildlife Service

U.S. Bureau of Reclamation

U.S. Bureau of Land Management—Oregon

U.S. Bureau of Land Management—California

The Resources Agency of California

California Energy Commission

California Biodiversity Council

Conservation organizations

The Nature Conservancy of California

The Nature Conservancy of Oregon

Foundations

The David and Lucile Packard Foundation

The Dean Witter Foundation

The Elizabeth and Stephen Bechtel Jr. Foundation

The Weiler Foundation

The Marshall Steel Sr. Foundation

Corporations

Cell Tech

Simpson Timber Company

Mastercard International

Second Nature Software

Individuals

William and Diane Zuendt
Richard and Angie Thieriot
Rig Currie and Trish Johnson
Hal Riney
Hal Nathan and Gail Seneca

As I traveled throughout the Klamath Basin conducting the photographic survey, many people shared their knowledge of the area. I am most grateful for their help. In particular, I would like to thank Jim Hainline, U.S. Fish and Wildlife Service; Jeff Mitchell, chairman of the Klamath Tribes; Wedge Watkins, Bureau of Land Management, Oregon; Ron Garrett, U.S. Fish and Wildlife Service (retired); Brian Woodbridge, U.S. Forest Service; and Phil Deitrich, U.S. Fish and Wildlife Service. Successful images were obtained also through the assistance of Craig Bienz and Larry Dunsmoor, Natural Resource Department, the Klamath Tribes; Bob Bell, U.S. Forest Service; Al McDermott and Rennie Cleland, California Department of Fish and Game; and Laurie Clark, U.S. Forest Service, Pacific Northwest Research Station.

To see and document the Klamath Basin from the air, I turned to the dedicated group known as Light Hawk and a very skilled pilot named Lew Nash. For the look back into Klamath Basin's past in the form of historical photographs, I received wonderful assistance from Pearl Nason and Patsy McMillan, director, Klamath County Museum; the Oregon Historical Society; and Aaron Ashurst, Ashurst Books, Klamath Falls, Oregon.

I want to express my appreciation to the University of California Press for their continued support of my work. To James H. Clark, director; Tony Crouch, production manager; Danette Davis, production coordinator; Rose Vekony, editor; and Steve Renick, designer, I thank you for taking five years of fieldwork and presenting it to the public in such a beautiful manner. The art of fine bookmaking is alive and well at the University of California Press.

For the long, dusty hours on bumpy logging roads, for calm sunsets filled with flying waterfowl, for frosty mornings and warm-woodstove, kitchen conversations with ranching families, I thank my friend and cohort, the writer of these wonderful essays, William Kittredge. I enjoyed the journey.

Last, I want to thank my wonderful wife, Madeleine. As a partner in photography, I enjoyed your gathering of black-and-white images of the people and the places it took us. As a partner in life, I forever appreciate your love and support.

TUPPER ANSEL BLAKE
Marsh Island Ranch
Klamath Basin, California

I was born in Klamath Falls and it was the place where I began my photographic career, in 1958, when I was ten, with a Kodak Starmite camera my dad gave me. I posed my cat alongside my ice skates and clicked. We left the area not long after the picture was made, and I never expected to return. But here I am, camera still in hand, only now it is a Hasselblad. What is different, also, is that I am here with a mind full of reference—and I see what a remarkable part of the world this is. I have been humbled and rewarded by my exploration of the people and place, and am grateful for the adventure.

My end of this project could not have been accomplished without the help of many people. Foremost, I would like to thank the people whose images appear in this book. They were gracious with their time and were cooperative, no matter what my requests.

I would like to specifically thank Becky Hatfield-Hyde for her assistance and friendship, Sharon and Don Rajnus for their introduction into the Czech community, Les and Linda Rexroat for persuading the buckaroos at the ZX that it would be OK for me to take some photos of them, and then driving me all over the place to get the pictures. Steve Spencer and Larry Murrell deserve thanks for help and sound advice, and Nancy Maltzan for the consistent warmth of her greeting. The gang at the Dorris post office—Danny Carlton, postmaster, Shelly Kujawski and Lori Schudda—has been great, with special thanks to Lori for her interface with the Hispanic community.

This project absolutely could not have been completed with the ease and joy that it was without the very fine darkroom facility, designed, built, and installed by J. Bradley Burns in my light-tight, mouse- and mosquito-free room built by Steve McKinney.

Special thanks go to Joan Lillivand, who, as it turns out, is an apt photo assistant, Susanna Henderson and Trish Johnson for their company during the project, and to Lillian Dickson, Peg Land, Barbara Burns, Rigdon Currie, and Boyd Watkins. I am also indebted to Don Worth, Jan Jambu, Jack Welpott, Alan Ross, and Art Rogers. And those of you not listed, please know my gratitude is deep.

To my parents, Steve and Cal Graham, I give the most grateful acknowledgment for patience, support, and love. And to my beloved husband, Tupper Ansel Blake, thank you so much for your great ideas and stoic persistence, and for reading in the evenings from Aldo Leopold's *A Sand County Almanac*.

For my part, I would like to dedicate this book to my son, Matt, and the memories of my mother and my grandmother.

Namaste,

MADELEINE GRAHAM BLAKE
Marsh Island Ranch
Klamath Basin, California

This book was Tupper Ansel Blake's idea. He got the project going, arranged for publication and financing, and then called me to ask if I'd like to take part in a watershed study of the Klamath Basin, where I'd gone to high school. Tupper and his wife, Madeleine, and I spent a lot of time together, and I enjoyed their company every step of the way. They are lovely people and immaculate artists.

We talked to a lot of people. Those I pestered the most were Linda Poole Rexroat, Gerta and John Hyde, Becky Hatfield-Hyde, Clinton Basey, Alice Kilham, Jim Carpenter, Wedge Watkins, Wendell Wood, Jim Hainline, Dan Byrne, Sam Henzel, Jack Liskey, Glenn Barrett, Mike Connelly, Elwood Miller, Jeff Mitchell, Bud Ullman, John Walker, Marshall Staunton, Carl Wenner, Louis Randall, the Bob and Eileen McKay family, Lee Juillerat, and Jim Kerns. They all were endlessly generous with their time and information. My friend Charles Wilkinson, an expert on Native American and western water law who is presently teaching at the University of Colorado School of Law, also gave me invaluable advice. Finally, all apologies to the people I've forgotten to thank.

Through my time on the book I tried to stay current on a maze of topical watershed matters by reading the *Klamath Falls Herald and News* and the bulletins released by the U.S. Fish and Wildlife Service, the Bureau of Reclamation, and other agencies, and by organizations like the Oregon Natural Resource Council and the Wilderness Society.

Reliable and comprehensive historical writing about the Klamath Basin is scarce. My main sources were *The Years of Harvest: A History of the Tule Lake Basin,* by Stan Turner (Eugene, Oregon: 49th Avenue Press, 1988); *The Klamath Project,* by Eric A. Stene (Denver: Bureau of Reclamation History Program, 1994); "Refuge Reclamation," by Doug Foster, *Southern Oregon Heritage* 1, no. 2 (fall 1995): 22–25; a typescript of "The Klamath Tribe: An Overview of Its Termination," by Kathleen Shaye Hill; *The Klamath Tribe: A People and Their Reservation,* by Theodore Stern (Seattle: University of Washington Press, 1965); *Cadillac Desert: The American West and Its Disappearing Water,* by Marc Reisner (New York: Viking, 1986); and *Rivers of Empire: Water, Aridity, and the Growth of the American West,* by Donald Worster (New York: Pantheon, 1985). Errors of fact or interpretation are of course my responsibility.

WILLIAM KITTREDGE
Missoula, Montana

Mallards,
Lower Klamath Lake,
California.

OTEY ISLAND

Pintails and mallards and teal in their quick undulating vee-shaped flights were everywhere in the early December twilight, wheeling and calling, setting their wings, settling. I was with Tupper Blake at the little property he calls Marsh Island Ranch. We were looking out over the Lower Klamath Lake National Wildlife Refuge. I was happy like a child.

Only a week or so before, Jim Hainline, head biologist at the Klamath National Wildlife Refuges, had flown the wetlands in the basin and estimated 3.7 million waterbirds, including 772,000 pintail ducks, 525,000 mallards, and slightly over 700,000 green-winged teals. Those were big numbers, way up from the annual fall count in recent years. Maybe the seemingly irreversible decline in the numbers of waterfowl using the refuges had stopped. Maybe the Pacific Flyway was coming back.

But in 1955 some 7 million waterbirds had been counted. And numbers on the Tule Lake side of the refuges now were disastrously low. By 1997 the Wilderness Society had listed the Klamath Basin refuges as one of the most endangered wild areas in the United States, saying, "Ecological survival is in doubt because of inadequate water supply, inappropriate farming and pesticides."

This is a story about watershed politics. It's about federal reclamation projects and farmers, cowhand ranchers and wildlife refuges, endangered suckers and bull trout and salmon, Native American tribespeople and hydroelectric dams and a little city, all wanting to use the same waters. People in the Klamath Basin of southern Oregon are irrevocably bound together by a system of flowing water. That water is their commons, the knot that holds them together while disputes over its uses drive them apart. The story here is about their attempts to solve intractable problems in communal and ultimately just ways. It is about their attempts to rethink the future, as people always have in the American West, in terms of watershed commonalities.

This is a story about conflict, people trying to preserve both their economic independence and remnants of what was once a sort of wildlands paradise—often quite contradic-

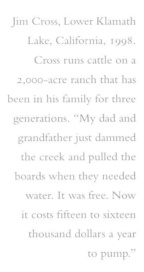

Jim Cross, Lower Klamath Lake, California, 1998. Cross runs cattle on a 2,000-acre ranch that has been in his family for three generations. "My dad and grandfather just dammed the creek and pulled the boards when they needed water. It was free. Now it costs fifteen to sixteen thousand dollars a year to pump."

tory purposes—trying to stave off irrevocable damage to both their communities and the natural world. It's about power, who has the switch. It's about trying to make a living, about bumper crops and $150,000 combines, about single mothers looking for work and families trying to feed their children without resorting to welfare, about toxic water in the marsh-land sumps and fish dying in an oxygen-depleted lake. It's about ditch-bank theorizing as to which is most important, the local economy or the health of the watershed—in the short run and in the long run—to both working people and the economically well established. And to the thronging world outside the basin.

Mistake it not, the great world has, particularly in the last decade, however local citizens may hate it, come to have a powerful and insistent say about affairs in the Klamath Basin. Increasingly, people everywhere think they have a stake in the Klamath ecosystem (they often don't show much concern about the economic system). They are willing to take that claim to the courts. Oftentimes they will win.

This is about people in the Klamath Basin taking stock of who they have been while trying to decide who they want to be. It's about deciding what kind of society they want. It's about people forced to decide what they want to call invaluable, never to be relinquished, which ideals and things, which ways of life, they will not consent to give up on or do without. It's a conjectural story about which of their often hard-earned personal economic prerogatives citizens in the basin will be called upon to give up, and which citizens will be most deeply involved in the giving. It's about trying to figure out how the processes of that giving will proceed. Because there's going to be some giving and some taking. Count on it. And probably lots of showdown blustering and courtroom anguishing no matter how it's done. Which can only be mitigated by the processes of civility, our ultimate commons. The Klamath Basin can be a model. If watershed problems can be confronted and solved in the Klamath Basin they can be solved in more complex watersheds, like the Columbia and the Colorado.

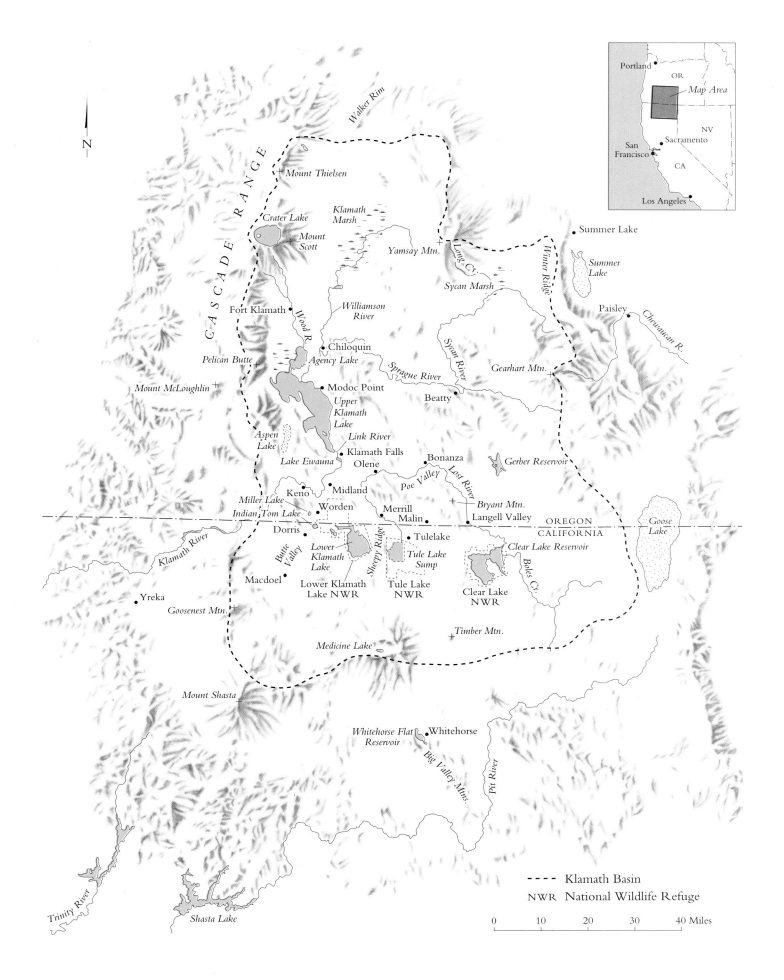

N

Walker Rim

CASCADE RANGE

+ *Mount Thielsen*

Klamath Marsh

Crater Lake

+ *Mount Scott*

Yamsay Mtn. +

Summer Lake •

Summer Lake

Long Cr.

Winter Ridge

Sycan Marsh

Paisley •

Chewaucan R.

Williamson River

Fort Klamath •

Wood R.

• Chiloquin

Agency Lake

Sycan River

Sprague River

Gearhart Mtn. +

Pelican Butte •

Mount McLoughlin +

• Modoc Point

Beatty •

Upper Klamath Lake

Aspen Lake

Link River

Lake Ewauna

• Klamath Falls
Olene •

• Bonanza

Gerber Reservoir

Poe Valley

Lost River

Keno •

• Midland

Bryant Mtn. +

Miller Lake
Indian Tom Lake

• Worden

Merrill •
Malin •

Langell Valley •

OREGON
CALIFORNIA

Goose Lake

Klamath River

• Dorris

Butte Valley

Sleepy Ridge

Lower Klamath Lake

• Tulelake

Tule Lake Sump

Clear Lake Reservoir

Lower Klamath
Lake NWR

Tule Lake
NWR

Boles Cr.

• Macdoel

Clear Lake
NWR

• Yreka

Goosenest Mtn. +

+ *Timber Mtn.*

Medicine Lake •

Mount Shasta

Whitehorse Flat Reservoir

• Whitehorse

Big Valley Mtns.

Pit River

Trinity River

Shasta Lake

- - - Klamath Basin

NWR National Wildlife Refuge

0   10   20   30   40 Miles

Portland •

OR

Map Area

NV

San Francisco •

• Sacramento

CA

Los Angeles •

"You can't eat nothing but birds," a dusty man told me. We were in a tavern on the fringes of the Tule Lake Basin. "Not for long. Pretty quick you people will find out you ate 'em all. Sooner or later you'll have to fall back on spud farmers."

He was a man who'd made his life in a country community based on irrigation agriculture. And now people from out of the basin wanted to take away a lot of the water and use it to fill swamps for ducks and geese, or just send it down the river, to the ocean, so the fish could thrive. Anybody with any sense of social responsibility, he seemed to think, anybody who worried about feeding exploding populations, would see such thinking as clear foolishness.

It's an old self-justifying farmer's argument, and sort of nonsensical in a world with massive food surpluses and falling commodity prices. But there was nothing to say that wouldn't get me into more of a confrontation than I wanted. He studied me; I sipped my drink. I had a degree of feeling for his emotions. At one time I'd seen farming as my life. In Warner Valley, not much more than a hundred miles to the east, I'd run irrigation water through a complicated system of canals and pumps, feeding it onto several thousands of acres of barley and alfalfa fields and then draining off the overflow. I loved that work. Close a single headgate, and you had to open another before the system overflowed. We called it "balancing water."

"Tell you what," I said. "Let me buy you a drink."

Another balancing act. Then I was out the door.

Seeing the actual birds, in the sky before us, was like confronting a sight of infinity, the earth, our only habitation, thronging with life.

Not long ago I heard a man point out that the lives of most citizens in the partway mechanical world we've invented for ourselves in recent centuries can be thought of as semi-denuded. Only in the last century has it been uncommon for people to witness wildlife spectacles. My great-grandfather saw millions of passenger pigeons over the forests of Kentucky. The last of them died in 1912, in the Cincinnati Zoo. My great-grandfather also traveled the Great Plains in the 1850s. Buffalo in thousands moved over the sandhill country of Nebraska, flowing over the grasslands like wind or waves on the sea. They were ordinary. Salmon thronged in rivers like the Klamath. We're a creature evolved to revere such sights, a hunting species. Life in such proliferation lights up our minds with visions of luck and, possibly, success. To me, *sacred* means that with which I will not consent to do without. Birds in the sky over Lower Klamath are to me sacred. The sight of life in its multitudes convinces me that I participate in a flow of meaningful energies, and that I am thus meaningful. It's a solacing notion, derived from witnessing life. It's about as religious as I get.

Tupper and I had parked at the foot of Otey Butte, a volcanic extrusion on his property, an inholding in the Lower Klamath Lake National Wildlife Refuge, and climbed the cou-

Swainson's hawks,
Butte Valley,
California.

ple of hundred feet to the top. In turn-of-the-century homestead days there was an orchard up there. We stepped over the remains of rock-work fences, laid up when Otey Butte was an island in a sea of tule marshes and reachable only by boat. Life for the men and women who settled on Otey Island must have been defined by hard work, and by sweat, and more work. And by dreams.

Northeast of the marshlands preserved by the waterfowl refuges are thousands of acres of ordered, irrigated, and drained farmlands. Beyond the agricultural lands are dry hills, which look much as they must have for millennia. Beyond them lie a thousand miles of mostly unbroken Great Basin deserts.

Tupper Blake came up from California and spent time and effort and money, turning his property, a second-rate hay and cattle ranch when he bought it, back into wetlands for the waterbirds. When local ranchers saw heavy equipment cutting imitation sloughs through fields that had once been laboriously drained, Tupper told them he was a "duckaroo." A lame joke, but it worked. Tupper's neighbors maybe thought he was crazy, but he loves the birds, and he was able to indulge his passion. Tupper knows what he wants and goes after it. His neighbors treat such dedication with respect. "It's like looking out over the ocean," Tupper said, from the top of Otey Butte. Thousands of birds were flying. "More animal hearts," he said, "than human hearts."

Maybe he's not so crazy. But then, he's not trying to make a living off farmland in the basin. Tupper and I are vastly privileged. We make our living as witnesses, a wildlife photographer and a writer. On Otey Butte, feeding on the natural glories, we were like tourists. We could, if not careful, respond primarily to our private inclinations to regard the birds as sacred. But it's important to recognize that local communities must be cared for in the same way that waterbirds are cherished. Protected with equal fervor.

EVERYTHING IS PART OF EVERYTHING

Tupper Blake tells of coming across a copy of Aldo Leopold's essays in a box of books while serving as a young army officer in Korea. He says, "I was sick of the officer's club and starved for something meaningful." Tupper tells of being illuminated by Leopold's concept of ecology, the insight that plants and animals, from bacteria to humankind, are absolutely interconnected, and that life on earth is an enormously complex, interwoven, irrevocably interdependent system. Tupper says Aldo Leopold's ideas formed his purposes: "I went into wildlife photography because of Aldo Leopold."

Aldo Leopold wrote, in his most fundamental formulation of his theories, "A thing is right when it tends to preserve the integrity, stability, and beauty of the biotic community. It is wrong when it tends otherwise." What Leopold means by "biotic community" is not simply individual plants and animals and species, but communal habitats, among them human habitats: farms and villages and neighborhoods, fields and marshes and metropolitan areas, all the vast variety of playing fields on which human life enacts itself. Leopold says ethics are based on the fact that each individual is and cannot help but be a member of a community of interdependent parts. He advocated what he called a "land ethic" based on the notion that preserving the biotic community is a fundamental human responsibility. The well-being of the worldwide biotic community is without doubt absolutely dependent on human conduct. We are the dominant species. Leopold was defining our responsibility for the well-being of endangered fish, and Tule Lake potato farmers, and ranchers in the Williamson River watershed, and for citizens who live in small towns like Merrill and Chiloquin, for unemployed timber fallers, and the insect communities in the Klamath marshlands. The entire biotic community that is life.

Those responsibilities resonate in the Klamath Basin, across the American West, and in China and Italy and Bolivia, everywhere. We are obliged to care for (1) evolving ecologies, and (2) each other, our various societies. We are obliged to care for "nature" and villages at the same time. Understood properly, it is the same agenda. There is, ethically, no other way to proceed.

Old growth, ponderosa pine,

Yamsay Mountain,

Oregon.

2

SYCAN MARSH

On a bright fall afternoon, Tupper and his wife, Madeleine, met me under the hill slopes of Winter Ridge, on the shores of Summer Lake. We stayed the night in a sweet bed-and-break-fast. We sampled the gin and ate brilliantly, a standing rib roast and the works. But in the morning some men wanted to tell us about their troubles with the Oregon Department of Fish and Wildlife, which owns and manages the wetlands at the north end of the lake. We didn't want to hear about it. Our purposes were over the ridge, in the Klamath country.

Westerners are used to spending their days out-of-doors and eager to get the action started. They don't sit well over reams of paperwork. We didn't want to hear about bureaucracies, we wanted to get on the road toward Sycan Marsh. We were rude and drove away. West-erners live in big country, with roads to travel; they get impatient and forget their manners. They have to be forgiven.

From Winter Ridge we looked east to the vast Great Basin deserts, then dropped over into timberlands. The logging roads, to my surprise, were mostly paved. We passed ghost trees left behind by the loggers, remnant stands of ponderosa, yellow pine; people in that country call them "big pumpkins," enormous and ancient, with open ground underneath, their tops often fractured by lightning strikes.

A quarter million acres of timbered watersheds slope to the meadows of Sycan Marsh. Once a shallow lake, Sycan was naturally sodded with deep peat soils over millennia, until it formed what was essentially a giant sponge. Until the end of the last century no water flowed out, but percolated into the earth, to reemerge in the downstream springs that fed the Sycan River. Then, a hundred years ago, the ZX Ranch started summering herds of cat-tle on Sycan. Visiting Sycan was like going back into the fringes of my own history.

The ZX, like the MC Ranch where I was a scab-handed boy, is an empire ranch in south-eastern Oregon. Headquartered in the town of Paisley, south of Summer Lake on the Chewaucan River marshes, it runs 11,000 mother cows and feeds another 12,000 to 14,000 calves each fall, and puts up 50,000 tons of hay. The ZX is presently regarded, at least in Oregon, as the largest operating cattle ranch in the United States.

The ZX is still a cowhand outfit, with around fifteen full-time horseback buckaroos. But a lot has changed. The ZX is now owned by the Simplot Corporation (potatoes for

Spring, Sycan Marsh,
Oregon.

Sandhill crane,
Sycan Marsh,
Oregon.

Ruddy duck,
Sycan Marsh,
Oregon.

McDonald's, the ranching properties, mining, frozen vegetables, computers, etc.), which
is headquartered in Boise. In 1980 Simplot sold 24,000 acres in the Sycan Marsh, while
retaining the right to lease the meadows and graze cattle there until the year 2020. The
Nature Conservancy was the buyer. The Conservancy is an organization dedicated to the
twin goals of preserving both the environment and agricultural lands. Some say these are
contrary purposes.

Linda Rexroat, the Nature Conservancy manager at Sycan Marsh, is not among them.
An energetic young woman who grew up on a horse ranch near Yakima, on the fringes of
the grasslands known as the Horse Heaven Hills, Linda is like a lot of us who recall our
childhood in terms of horseback days in open country across the West. Many of us tend to
think of that childhood as our personal version of an innocent, intimate, natural paradise.
I do, anyway. So does Linda. By the time she was off to Evergreen College in Olympia for
a degree in environmental science, the little ranch where she grew up had been sold and
subdivided. "I almost can't bear it," she says, "to go there and look. Houses everywhere."

These circumstances have a great deal to do with her powerful allegiance to the preservation of open land and, to some degree, explain her emotional affinity for the horseback
culture embodied by the ZX cowhands. It's a dual heritage that has helped her get along.
After getting her master's degree in wildlife science from Oregon State University, when
she came to Sycan Linda married a former ZX cow boss, Les Rexroat, who has become the
get-the-work-done man for the Conservancy. His presence carries authority with the ZX
cowhands. Their cooperation in Linda's work is essential. "But it's more than that. Les keeps

ZX buckaroos: Mark
Williams, cow boss; Bill
Gladwill, Gilbert Camarillo,
Mike Merchant, and
Chris Hunt, Sycan Marsh
Preserve, Oregon, 1998.

me straight," Linda says. "When I get discouraged, he tells me to sit my ass down in the saddle." Which is a variation on a metaphor we heard a lot in the Klamath country. Get down, work close, if you want to understand a place, its citizens and climates and creatures. Farm and ranch families take pride in an intimate knowledge of their territory. As do Native American people. It's a notion environmentalists, in their scientific language, also endorse. Without paying absorbed attention to the details, the processes of life and how they interact, how one triggers another, we'll never fathom the flow of energies that constitute a place.

Much of the controversy in the West—between farmers and ranchers, agency bureaucrats, scientists, tribal citizens, and environmentalists—is a result of people speaking different versions of what is thought to be a common language. Talk is degraded into a posturing, adversarial game. We quit listening, and only talk to those we agree with, who speak "our language." We find ways to continue disagreeing. Soon, someone calls a lawyer. It's Linda's job to balance the demands of restoring the marshland ecosystem at Sycan—severely degraded by decades of careless water management and overgrazing, in places eroded into deep gullies and dead scablands, the peat soils long gone—and the day-to-day grazing needs of the Simplot Corporation. The first thing she had to do was get the cow people from the ZX and Conservancy scientists talking the same language. "Without the cooperation of the ZX," Linda says, "we were dead in the water."

The terms of the Simplot/Conservancy grazing lease had to be renegotiated. "In order to get anywhere we had to reduce the number of animals summering on the marsh." But

Linda and Les Rexroat, Sycan
Marsh, Oregon, 1998.

ranchers in the West have heard a lot of that kind of talk in recent years. It was a good bet the ZX would never buy in. "We were fortunate," Linda says. "Simplot was cooperative. They agreed to seriously cut the numbers grazing on the marsh for a few years. We had to give the place a chance to respond to the recovery plan." If the plan worked, the ZX would eventually be able to run more animals than before the agreement on better grass. "It was a deal in which everybody could win." So far it's working.

By the end of this decade, barring unforeseeable disaster, Sycan will be growing more grass, and the ZX will be summering more animals there. Linda gives credit for success to a man named Bob DeBraga, manager of the ZX at the time. "We got started," she said, "by trying to understand the on-the-ground environmental complexity. Both environmentalists and cowboys are into that. Grazing isn't inherently destructive. Cows and grasslands and water just have to be managed in mutually beneficial ways."

They got results. Linda likes to show photographs of eroded scablands in the heart of Sycan, then take visitors for a walk through knee-high grass on the same acreage. In 1996 Linda Rexroat won the National Wetlands Conservationists Award for Individual Accomplishment from the United States Fish and Wildlife Service. In February of 1998, she won the Outstanding Achievement Award from the Society for Range Management, an organization with members in forty-eight countries. "So maybe we're getting something done," she says. Her pride seems justifiable. "It wasn't me," she says. "It was all of us, our work."

Results on Sycan Marsh imply that a lot of the trouble between agriculturalists and environmentalists is driven by the energies of territoriality: who gets to call the shots in mat-

Bull trout,
Long Creek,
Oregon.

ters centered too often on nothing more than lingo and so-called lifestyles. Ego problems. If citizens trying to talk to one another are attempting to be useful, they begin with much the same basic agenda: How to take care? Practical problems often can be worked out if the people involved are trying to solve them and not just defeat one another, and if they are paying attention to messages coming back from the biological health of the land.

Certainly that's the story the Nature Conservancy would like us to take away from Sycan Marsh. But some problems won't yield to compromise. Linda is facing one at Sycan. Standing above Long Creek, which flows into Sycan from the west, Linda breaks out photographs to document the recovery of what is called the riparian area. Thick stands of grass and small willows have returned to stream banks once tromped to bare mud by cattle. The cut-bank erosion is in check. It's another success story. But Long Creek is a spawning ground for bull trout, which have lately been listed as threatened under the federal Endangered Species Act. Which means ZX cows will have to be fenced entirely away from the water. Linda will be in charge. Her flexibility is diminished, and her hard-earned relationship with the ZX is threatened. "What's more important," I asked, "the survival of a species or the well-being of the Simplot Corporation?"

Linda gave me a look. "That's not," she said, "how it is." If not, hard-line enviros will ask, how is it? Hard-line enviros are a lot more interested in the survival of the species than the well-being of some corporate entity.

"If you want to help things get better," Linda says, "sometimes you have to work with the people who own them." Linda Rexroat is a hard-working realist. She's respected everywhere in the Klamath country for representing both environmental and ranch interests with balance and good judgment. She ought to be. Not many people could do her job.

YAMSI

From Sycan, Tupper, Madeleine, and I drove through timberlands to the headwaters of the Williamson River, where it wanders in pretty meadows. We were headed for the Hyde Ranch, the setting for a good book called *Yamsi*, named after the timbered mountain off to the northeast. The book was written by Dayton Hyde, who was raised on the property by his uncle Buck Williams.

In *Yamsi*, Hyde tells of his responsibility for the place and local creatures: "Without me a uniquely primitive and irreplaceable environment will die, the lonely sanctuary, the home of the owl and eagle, osprey, kingfisher, and crane." Strong feelings, but it's never up to just one of us. And Dayton Hyde is gone, off to manage a herd of wild horses on properties in South Dakota. His wife, Gerda, and their children, and their children's families, have taken responsibility for the land along the Williamson River.

Gerda Hyde is one of the matriarchs in the Klamath country. When she greeted us, she was dressed for work in the fields, taking time out from putting up hay. "It's what there is," she said about the work, combing her fingers through her mane of vivid gray hair. Gerda is devoted to her family and the place, a conservationist and a traditionalist. Over the years she's planted 5,000 willows along the banks of the Williamson and 250,000 other trees, ponderosa and jack pine.

Gerda made it clear she didn't trust me or what I might write about the life she reveres. "Don't you talk about us," she said, "like you did about your family." My family, from 1916 until quite recently, owned a place just down the river from the Hyde Ranch. I think members of my family suffered an overdeveloped desire to own properties, and that they acted on that desire in oftentimes ruthless ways, and I've said so. They were people Gerda knew, and admired, at least for their courage, their ability to endure. She thought, as I read her, that I had betrayed them and, in that betraying, attacked all ranchers.

So I ducked my head. Gerda lives in an elegant arts-and-crafts house, stonework and burnished hardwood, among yellow pine overlooking the Williamson River (counting turns, the ranch has eight miles of river frontage). The house was built in the days when the only way in from town was horseback or a couple of days in a wagon, by Buck Williams, a man

"It is fortunate, perhaps, that no matter how intently one studies the hundred little dramas of the woods and meadows, one can never learn all of the salient facts about any one of them."

Spring, Williamson River,
Oregon.

Becky Hatfield-Hyde,
Callie Hyde holding
Elizabeth Hyde, and Gerda Hyde,
Yamsi Ranch, Williamson
River, Oregon, 1998.

whose idea of a kingdom in the wilderness seemed to center on concepts of a balance between wildness and civility. These people, so far as I knew, were not afflicted by the ac-
quisitiveness that gripped my family. At the same time they seemed determined to care for
themselves, their place to live, and their way of living there.

Tupper and Madeleine and I stayed across the lawns in the guest house. Pilgrims pay a
serious fee to stay at the ranch and enjoy catch-and-release fly-fishing on the Williamson
River, for rainbows, and for brook trout talked about as the largest in Oregon. Visitors come
from places like Australia and England. Some of those lunker trout must have been caught
dozens of times.

Gerda brought fresh sheets and insisted on making up beds for us. Tourist businesses, no
matter how they're dressed, come down to serving others. But it's not a bad way of making a living, even with the wear and tear on the fish. At the Hydes', I think, it's predicated
on spreading the pleasure around.

A half dozen of us sat down to dinner that night, Gerda and her oldest son, John, and
his brother, Taylor, a veterinarian who specializes in livestock, and Taylor's young wife, Becky
Hatfield-Hyde.

John Hyde is responsible for running the ranch, and he's fed up with the red tape and paperwork, the slow-as-molasses decision-making processes he's involved with as he deals with
state and federal bureaucracies. His complaints center on administrative incoherence and bad
or ill-timed actions and policies, as well as simple gridlock inefficiency. Farmers and ranchers say things like "Damn the bureaucracies. All they do is build their little tin kingdoms.

And triple damn their paperwork." Some complaints are just the griping of people whose ancestors went West seeking territory, freedom, and economic possibility. Rural West-erners, who have lived in isolation and thus had their own way for a long time, often and understandably hate the idea of answering to governmental regulatory agencies staffed by educated but locally inexperienced outsiders. Westerners, like all of us, want simple, clean answers to their problems. And there most often aren't any. Answers to on-the-ground difficulties are usually complex, and many take years to emerge.

But the problem with bureaucracies is real. Responses to environmental problems are of-ten best made on the spot, before bothering with paperwork. Bureaucratic decision-making is too slow for the responsible management of complex and quickly evolving ecologies. People who live inside an ecosystem know this. And they often know how to solve the problems. But their hands are legally tied, and it can take a bureaucracy, particularly one lo-cated thousands of miles away, a long time to respond. Then agencies often respond in overly image-conscious ways. Locals want the agencies to be stable and sensible and reliable, staffed by people who understand local particularities, capable of making swift decisions and, at the same time, willing to advocate slow-growing programs that may take decades to work out but that don't wreck local economies.

John Hyde is dismayed by United States Forest Service fire suppression policies, which encourage brushy undergrowth on the timbered ridges above the Williamson River. Bu-reaucrats are traditionally afraid of burning because fires, as in the example of Yellowstone a few years back, might flare out of control and create a public relations disaster. Histori-

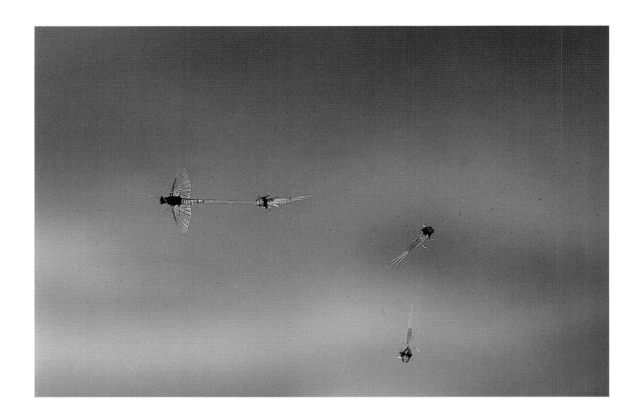

cally, responding to the will of the public, they've put out fires, natural and otherwise. But wildfires, however dangerous, are essential to the evolution of forest ecologies. Traditional Indian cultures knew this and set fires every autumn to encourage regrowth and provide good browse and grazing for the hunting animals. Buck Williams came to the country and found he could drive wagons through the open parks under the great yellow pine. Now it's hard to ride a horse across those same brushy hills.

"There's no point in putting out fires. There's no point in keeping things the way they are," John Hyde said. "What we have to do is take care of uplands, not just the streams. We have to bring back the diversity. That's the true goal. The snow won't hold in that brush. Used to be, big drifts would pack in and last until spring. Now they bleed away. The uplands are absolutely dried out by August. One day we're going to have a holocaust fire."

It's easy to imagine. The hill slopes above the meadows by the Williamson River are thick with downed timber that should have burned off decades ago. John Hyde, talking from his point of view as a rancher, was sounding like an environmentalist.

But until ranchers and farmers and agency employees stop harping on matters of fault and blame, give up adversarial ways of going at one another, they're going to have a tough time solving their problems in any sort of cooperative and workable manner. Nothing is likely to change until the citizenry makes up its mind. Then locals lead, politicians and bureaucrats follow, and change comes quickly, oftentimes easily.

Watershed study groups, mostly made up of farmers and ranchers working out solutions to their own difficulties, are a popular political-problem-solving model in the contemporary

West. Becky Hatfield-Hyde comes from a ranch family well-known for their efforts to bring grazing interests and environmentalists together to solve mutual problems. In 1990 her parents, Doc and Connie Hatfield, got ranchers together with scientists from the Bureau of Land Management in an effort to preserve endangered Lahontan cutthroat trout in a tiny landlocked stream in the Whitehorse Mountains of southeastern Oregon. Years of talk were involved, a lot of give-and-take. The result was a management success. Cows were kept out of riparian areas. The trout made a comeback, to the point where they may no longer be listed as endangered. And ranchers are still grazing cattle in the Whitehorse Mountains. The process worked for two reasons. Faced with the inflexible demands of the Endangered Species Act, ranchers knew they had to change their practices or lose their grazing rights. Second, the Hatfields are informed and respected locals, ranchers, and conservationists and are willing to be long-term leaders. They could keep the talk going. And they recognized the inevitability of change.

But a similar effort didn't come to much for ranchers on the upper Williamson River. In the first place, there didn't seem to be so much at stake. The ranchers, John Hyde and others, hoped to build fences in the timberlands beside their meadows in order to adopt the intensive grazing practices advocated by Alan Savory and his Holistic Range Management Institute (improving the range by imitating natural ungulate grazing patterns, grazing on small areas for a short, intensive time, then moving on, as bison do). The idea was worth trying, but working out the details was not absolutely urgent to the ranchers or the Forest Service. No natural leaders emerged. Both ranchers and bureaucrats had more pressing agendas elsewhere. After facing the initial paperwork, the Williamson River Watershed Working Group soon quit meeting.

But locals, John Hyde says, have always talked to one another, working out practical problems in practical ways. The agencies must streamline their processes, and they must learn to make citizens welcome; they must earn reputations as amiable and trustworthy if not always acquiescent. What the agencies might do, Hyde thinks, is hire ranchers and farmers, people who ordinarily care for the places where they live, and make them responsible for solving problems. Monitor them closely, demand, and pay for, results. "We've got to get beyond warfare. All the agencies do is blow the whistle. They could be using ranchers as tools. Why not hire locals to do conservation work, the people who have the most to gain?"

It's a notion many conservationists would regard with profound distrust. Federal agencies, they'd say, aren't responsible for local economies; agency employees are hired to protect the nation's environment, nothing else. We'd hear about foxes in the henhouse, things like "Ranchers trash wild areas. Then we pay them to do restorative work."

But, driven by public will, as an enactment of responsibility for common property, it could work. Eventually, some such scheme will work. Public will is going to demand that farmers and ranchers and conservationists and bureaucrats stop posturing and get down to work solving their mutual problems, which are complex but not in any way insolvable. Common use problems will be solved, as they have been in the highland grazing pastures of Switzerland and the terraced rice lands of Java, all over the earth, for thousands of years, by citizens willing to recognize what has to be done and then doing it, by applications of common local sense. It's beginning to happen in the Klamath Basin. Which is our story here.

Williamson River,
Klamath Marsh,
Oregon.

3

THE MARSH

We knew it as "the Marsh," a tract of hay fields and grazing lands my family owned along the upper Williamson River, downriver from the Yamsi Ranch. Seven thousand years ago it was a shallow lake filled with pumice by the explosion of Mount Mazama, which had formed Crater Lake. Over millennia the grasses and tules rotted and built deep peat soils.

My grandfather started grazing cattle on the marsh in 1911, leasing land from members of the Klamath tribes, to whom this land, as part of the Klamath Reservation, belonged. He began buying up allotments from tribespeople in 1916, and selling off timber from the fringes of the meadows to pay for the land. One winter he traded a wagon load of groceries for a quarter section. At least that's the story. Much of what he got was marsh, flooded most of the year and of not much apparent value. But he made it pay. After excavating a drainage ditch with an apparatus called an elevating grader, pulled by a sixteen-mule hitch, he was able to dry up considerable acreage to be hayed. The list of his fields makes a sort of poetry: Cholo, Hog Island, Brick Jim, Association, and Abraham Flat. Know the stories behind those names and you'd know more local history than I do. It's going to be mostly lost after another generation passes.

In the fall of 1967, riding after my family's cattle (we were getting out of the cow business), I would rest my horse among yellow pine at a place called Sagebrush Point. The snowy peaks of the Cascades were silhouetted on the skyline to the west. A few waterbirds would be flying. When I was old enough to want tranquillity, I thought, I'd come back and build a house, and live in that house until death. The first home my parents took me to, for my first winter on earth, was the Mayfield Place, just a few miles upriver. It's been abandoned for a long time.

Mornings in my imaginary house at Sagebrush Point I'd be able to see to the absolute edge of things while getting used to the idea of dying. Birds in the spring, fields of glazed snow. Binoculars on the windowsill. That was the idea.

But we live more lives than one. My home is in Montana. I'll never build that house at Sagebrush Point. Which is all right. Those properties are now owned and managed by the U.S. Fish and Wildlife Service. Seventy or so pairs of sandhill cranes nest on the marsh, and

Tule geese,
Klamath Marsh,
Oregon.

spring flights of ducks and geese from Mexico and California rest there before heading north to nest in the tundra.

Clinton Basey was the man who saw to getting the work done in 1967, as winter came down. We tied panty hose over our ears, and our horses skated on ice and frozen sod. My brother and I hung back while Basey rode those slick meadows full tilt. We would have been helpless without him.

On a bright day in the fall of 1997 I went back to visit Clinton and his wife, Mary Anne. Down at the blacksmith shop, I tapped a hammer on an anvil and fell into recalling days in which reverence for the enduring rhythms of animals and work seemed to stitch things together. Thirty years had got away. But the old fire-hardened juniper corral posts were as solid as ever, and Clinton and Mary Anne were as located in the particularities of the day as they had been when I saw them last. I talked, and Clinton smiled and said, "You got as much wind as you ever had."

On brilliant autumn afternoons I can still go sit by the yellow pine on Sagebrush Point, listening to woodpeckers in the timberland while the sky above the Cascade peaks turns toward twilight. It would be a way of ignoring time and the great world, as potent a solace against oncoming darkness as any experience I could find anywhere. The rhythms of everything would be going on without me. As they will.

Clinton Basey, ranch
manager, Klamath Marsh,
Oregon, 1998.

THE STATE OF KLAMATH

Klamath, for me, is a country thick with ghosts, stories about people who have been dead for decades. I grew up in southeastern Oregon, and more than forty years ago I went to high school in Klamath Falls. In my motel room during December of 1997, doing research on this book, I would study the obituary columns in the *Klamath Herald and News,* looking to see if anyone I knew had died, and, if so, what they had made of their lives. It had come to that. The cure, as usual, was the future. People on the streets laughed as they made ready to celebrate Christmas. They were, and are, bound together in a common enterprise, taking care of our only possible home, the sweet and watered earth, and its creatures, including ourselves.

The Klamath Basin is a homeland for a nation of spud farmers, downtown clerks, log truck drivers, real estate brokers and schoolteachers, hippy mothers and civil engineers, computer nuts and Klamath Indians, agribusiness capitalists, out-of-work millwrights, cutting-horse fanciers, retired escapees from California, and a few hard-core conservationists. Who's left out? Everybody, in the particularity of their dreams. Nobody can be named so simply. We aren't any of us like anybody else in our private triumphs, in our woundings and yearnings. Yet we have to live together.

The Klamath Basin is an empire of timberlands (mostly logged) and wetlands (down from about 350,000 acres in the basin prior to 1900) and fecundity. From Crater Lake, situated on the ridge of the Cascades, from Yamsay Mountain and the jack pine flats north of Sycan Marsh, the Klamath watershed flows south into country cupped like the palm of a vast, open hand.

The Williamson River and the Sycan River and the Sprague rise from mountains to the north. The Wood River bubbles up from the sandy bottom of a great perpetual spring. They each meander through timberland meadows and marshes, into the shallow expanses of Klamath Lake, said to be the largest freshwater lake in the American West. There, the waters historically rested at the heart of the territory. Natural overflow moved into the Link River (the shortest river in the United States) near Klamath Falls and fell to Lake Ewauna (for a hundred years degraded into a millpond on the edge of the city). The waters emerge renamed, as the Klamath River, which flows to the Pacific. Water from the Klamath River backed into Lower Klamath Lake in high-water periods and flowed out in times of low water; and

Above: The steamboat *Klamath* moved freight and people between California and Oregon, circa 1907. Courtesy of The Klamath County Museum.

A freight wagon crosses the Klamath River. Courtesy of The Klamath County Museum.

Lost River flowed through marshlands into Tule Lake, where it was naturally impounded. Over millennia, through dry seasons and wet, as the water came and went, tules grew and rotted.

White-water trout streams and rivers flowing into the vast shallow lake where the great sucker fish lived, and then to marshlands where waterbirds nested, into the Klamath River where salmon spawned, then into the canyon that fell between forested mountains to the Pacific—this was the Klamath country when the white people came. Wagon-train settlers seeking agricultural land, after laboring along the Applegate Trail across the alkaline flatlands of the Great Basin, the Black Rock Desert of Nevada, and up over Fandango Pass and into Oregon, must have smelled the boggy water and rotting tules before they came over the last hilltop through the junipers to gaze down on the dark swamps edging Tule Lake. Shasta, the imperial snowy mountain, loomed on the horizon, white against a sky so blue it looked breakable, the mountain a vision of purity, like some crystalline heaven.

Those settlers had located a dream, and a home. The Klamath country must have looked

White-faced ibis,
Lower Klamath Lake,
California.

like the happy land where their expectations could come to realization. Some of those travelers must have imagined life in a white-painted house, their children and grandchildren running through a blossoming orchard, a bright endlessness of water running in their ditches, green plow-ground fields.

White settlement proceeded and natural processes in the Klamath watershed were transformed. Eighty percent of the 185,000 acres of marshlands and shallow lakes in the southern end of the basin were drained (about 36,000 acres are left). Seven dams were built, as were eighteen canals reaching 185 miles, 516 miles of lateral ditch, and forty-five pumping plants. As might be expected in such an extensive reworking, natural processes began to fail, to malfunction. Various creatures began falling through the cracks. Waterfowl numbers in the basin, because of habitat destruction in the basin and elsewhere up and down the Pacific Flyway, fell to around 15 percent of what they had been. Over 100 of 411 vertebrate species in the Klamath Basin are now classified as sensitive, threatened, or endangered. Salmon are cut off from their spawning beds by hydroelectric dams on the Klamath River. This, together with siltation by runoff from badly logged hill slopes, and overfishing, primarily accounts for their precipitous decline. Something has to be done. In how many ways can we define wealth?

The Klamath-Trinity, at its mouth, due to enormous coastal rainfall, is the third largest stream-flow system on the western coast of the United States. But upstream in southern Oregon, the Klamath isn't large enough. A hundred and fifty years after the first settlers

Snow geese and cackling
Canada geese, Tule Lake,
California.

found what seemed to be an infinity of water, there isn't enough late-season water, at least in dry years. In 1992 and in 1994, there wasn't enough water to maintain the marshlands with their waterbirds, and the lakes and rivers with their endangered fishes, and traditional agriculture. It's likely to happen again.

Blame El Niño, global warming, gases emitted by industries. Ultimately the allocation and uses of water, its pollution, and the shortfalls are the ranking problems in the Klamath Basin. They will not, in any foreseeable future, go away. But perhaps if the citizens of the basin are persistent and resilient, those problems will over time drive them to a reinvented sense of communality.

In fantasy, the Klamath Basin could be its own political entity, like a state, with elected officials and a legislature and a state seal, in charge of solving its own problems. It's a notion John Wesley Powell would have endorsed. Powell was born in New York in 1834, lost the lower part of his right arm at the battle of Shiloh in the Civil War, and went on to become a leading western scientific surveyor and explorer. He is famous for leading the initial expedition down the Grand Canyon in 1869. On May 24 his expedition left Green River, Wyoming, with nine men in four dories. Strapped into a captain's chair with no life vest or any possibility of rescue, Powell ran rapids with fifty-foot waves and lost his scientific instruments when his boat capsized. His journals, bound in leather, were saved. Six survivors came out of the canyon at a Mormon fishing camp near the Virgin River after ninety-nine days.

John Wesley Powell became obsessed with defining the connection between the proper use of water and settlement in the desert lands of the West. He spent thirteen years as head of the United States Geological Survey. In his *Report on the Lands of the Arid Region of the United States,* published in 1878, he proposed that settlement in the West be based on impounding wild rivers and on the use of stored water for irrigation. Otherwise, he said, there was not enough water in the West to support civilization. These notions seemed prophetic during the disastrous three-year western drouth a decade later (1888, 1889, and 1890). People who had made their homes in the dry West were forced to acknowledge that the notion of rain following the plow, an idea promoted by developers in the interest of attracting settlers, was a preposterous fraud.

Powell was intent, according to the historian Donald Worster in *Rivers of Empire: Water, Aridity, and the Growth of the American West,* on "redeeming" the West by damming rivers that were "running to waste." Powell envisioned "complete domination of nature." Streambeds should be drained dry, so that not a drop of water would escape. Starting with the National Reclamation Act of 1902 (the year Powell died), this recommendation has been vigorously acted out in the West. The vast irrigation projects in the lower end of the Klamath Basin are in part a result of Powell's vision.

Goshawk, Goosenest
Mountain, California.

But Powell had another, more radical idea that went nowhere. He thought political entities in the arid West should be defined by watershed boundaries rather than straight lines
on a map. Powell understood that communities in the West are inevitably drawn together
by shared watershed interests.

But "hydraulic societies" often end up with some variety of totalitarian government.
Powell understood. He wrote that "in the practice of agriculture by irrigation in high an-
tiquity, men were organized as communal bodies or as slaves to carry on such labor by united
labor. Thus the means of obtaining subsistence were of such a character to give excuse and
cogent argument for the establishment of despotism." In short, it takes a chain of command
to run a large project, a power structure, usually in the form of a continuing, self-replacing
bureaucracy. It's true in both governments and corporations. No matter how benevolent in
the beginning, over time bureaucracies tend to become despotisms, empires, complete with
privileged hierarchies. From the ancient Near East to the recent Communist experiment,
they have tended to be increasingly antidemocratic, inflexible, and dysfunctional. But, Powell said, that pattern could not develop in the American West, because there "the love of
liberty is universal."

Because the impetus behind it would be the desire to locate or create good farmland for
people seeking liberty and opportunity, technologically organized irrigation in the American West would, according to Powell, provide an economic basis for the development of
a semi-classless yeoman democracy—farmers and ranchers, small towns, irrigation com-

munities. The Jeffersonian agenda. The arid West, which Powell defined as lying west of the one-hundredth meridian (excluding the well-water lands of the Pacific Northwest and Northern California), comes to 1,340,000 square miles. Governance boundaries in that area, Powell said, should be drawn along watershed boundaries, forming "natural districts." Water rights should be unalterably fused to local control. Each "natural district" would be a "commonwealth within itself." One hundred million acres could be "redeemed," land for a million and a quarter family farms. How to ensure that a semi-classless, inherently democratic society did indeed evolve? Here, Powell's practicalities drift into what was widely regarded as an idealistic dream.

In Powell's scheme, families would be limited to 80 acres of irrigated land within the district. Ranchers would stop making free use of the public domain; timber companies would not be allowed to buy up forested federal lands. So-called means of production would be secure in the hands of small operators, families, and not national or international corporations. Powell was advocating cooperation, rationality, scientific development, and the equitable sharing of natural wealth. Fat chance. It was a notion of society that didn't play very well in the essentially wide-open and winner-take-all adversarial economic battlefield that was shaping up in the gold camps and on the ranges and timber- and farmlands of the West.

A lot of frustration for local citizens has come of ignoring, or at least not working seriously toward, the democratic essence of John Wesley Powell's idea about watershed states. The Klamath Basin, as environmental and economic problems play out, has a chance of becoming a war zone—nobody wins but the lawyers. We hope the human urge toward honoring communality will in the long run win the day. That honoring will involve transforming ways people in the Klamath Basin habitually think about their community and reimagining notions of self-governance. Such rethinking won't come easy.

Increasingly, like it or not, cultures are homogenized: we live in an international commons. And it will be a commons in the end, count on it. Rich and happy, or exploited and denuded. The options stand open. Practical people who live in the Klamath Basin are developing homegrown political entities on the model proposed so long ago by John Wesley Powell. They are trying to solve local and regional problems within a framework of federal and state regulations, using local expertise. It's a tall order. They are inventing, whatever they call it, an actual functioning State of Klamath. The processes, created as they go, can and will be subverted and exploited at every juncture. But it's the only game in town. The story of our time, in the Klamath Basin and the West, is about unavoidable responsibilities, learning to care for and repair the commonalities we inhabit, both in nature and in our economies, our human communities.

Chinook salmon,

Klamath River,

California.

4

TIME IMMEMORIAL

The Hupa people along the downstream reaches of the Klamath-Trinity River system lived in small villages. They built cedar-plank houses with central hearths, over oblong pits. Each village also had a large ceremonial house.

The center of their world was at the junction of the Klamath and Trinity Rivers, the village called Weitchpec. The key to their existence was the life cycle of the Chinook salmon. Each year, in the fall, an enormous run of salmon came from the sea and went upriver to their spawning beds. The Hupa, together with tribes called Yurok and Karok, constructed a huge fishing weir a few miles downstream from Weitchpec.

World-renewal ceremonies to encourage the return of the spawning Chinook took place over a period of fifty days before the construction of the weir. Building the weir took ten days. It was allowed to stand for ten days. During that time the people harvested much of their yearly supply of protein from the river. Then the weir was dismantled so upstream people could take their share of the salmon run.

It is estimated that the Indians took a million pounds of salmon from the river each year. How many Chinook in a million pounds? Twenty-five thousand if the fish are enormous, like the old so-called native hogs that came upstream to spawn in the Columbia. Try to imagine twenty-five thousand huge fish in ten days. Twenty-five hundred salmon every day. How many fishermen? Why can't I stop counting? (It's said putting numbers on glory is a pimp's job.)

What I yearn to see, in the eye of my mind, is the greenish river rolling and surging through the rocky defile, the great weir, and hook-jawed red-and-green spawner Chinooks leaping toward their fates, and fishermen with their fish. The tearing down of the weir when they had enough. The simple, slippery interconnections. Sounds sexual. Reproductive.

The Hupa knew that processes we call natural are sacred; people cannot exist without them. They thought that everything was alive, everywhere, all of it, and that the living processes would reward us for living well, that taking care, thus honoring life, was the prime way of earning what we call good luck. The Hupa way of thinking was ancient, part of a religion that anthropologists call animism. At its center is the notion that all things, not just

Early salmon fishing on the Klamath River. Photograph by Telford. Courtesy of The Klamath County Museum.

those that are in some way humanly informed, are sacred. Hupa lives involved ceremonies, and reverence, giving in order to get. Recently, their days involve lawyers. They want the power to control their fate.

The American West has historically been an emotional, intellectual, and economic colony of the East and Europe. Men and women intent on colonizing, everywhere, from Oregon to Abyssinia, have been intent on takeover, conquest of original inhabitants. The conduct of colonists has always tended to display profoundly racist tendencies. The history of European conquest, we know, is often a story of slavery, genocide, and commercial exploitation. There are plenty of examples. Colonialist Europeans in Africa, Asia, Australia, Mexico, South America, and the American West most often treated native people like weeds, to be weeded. Or to be moved onto reserves, out of the way, so mercantilist civilization could proceed on its long march. These attitudes were understood as necessary to progress, which was defined as movement toward the colonist's own economic well-being, which in turn centered on owning the land and, as a sort of afterthought, the water.

Until gold was discovered in country traditionally occupied by the Hupa and their neighbors along the Klamath River in the 1850s, those people lived in traditional ways. But then miners swarmed through the river valleys, and the sacred life in the timbered canyons was dismantled. The results were catastrophic disease and poverty.

The question that resonates in every indigenous society, particularly those conquered and victimized in the centuries of colonialism: How to live in accord with your beliefs when they are not shared or honored by the dominant culture—when they are regarded as ridiculous?

The answer, these days: Hire some lawyers. Or better yet, encourage your brightest young people to attend the best law schools in the nation. Tribal people along the Klamath River didn't invent the battleground that is the American court system. But they have to fight their battles there. So they are preparing. Whites, they say, can't blame them.

Frozen marsh,
Upper Klamath Lake,
Oregon.

Native people have lived in the Klamath country since time immemorial. Stories about the explosion of Mount Mazama, which created Crater Lake six thousand years ago, tell of the sun vanishing behind clouds of ash. Pumice, light enough to float once it cooled, rained everywhere.

People thought everything had ended. For many it had. That explosion is understood as the first great catastrophe. The second catastrophe, many thousands of years later, was the coming of the white people. Ordinary life took place in the vast run of seasons in between, people fishing and gathering and hunting, grieving for their dead and celebrating birth and rebirth.

The Klamath country before white settlement was inhabited by small and distinct, village-based tribal political entities known to themselves as marsh people, river people, lake people, the far-off people (who lived south of Tule Lake), the nomadic Yahooskin (Paiute) peoples from the edge of the northern Great Basin, and groups from the Pit River country of California. They seem to have had little contact with the downriver cultures of the Yurok, Karok, or Hupa.

The Klamath people, estimated to number about eight hundred, settled for the winter in villages of subterranean earth lodges, entered by means of ladders through a hole in the roof, on the Klamath Marsh, along the Williamson River, on the east shores of Agency and Upper Klamath Lakes, and beside the Link River. Modoc villages, home to about four hundred people, lay around Lower Klamath, Tule, and Clear Lakes, as well as alongside the Lost River.

"*The land ethic simply enlarges the boundaries of the community to include soils, waters, plants, and animals, or collectively: the land.*"

Wind-driven ice floe,
Tule Lake,
California.

On the banks of the Lost
River, members of the
Klamath tribes dry a species
of fish they called *c'wam* (Lost
River sucker), circa 1898.
Photograph by Maud
Baldwin. Courtesy of The
Klamath County Museum.

During the warmer seasons the Klamath were quite nomadic. Soon as winter ice began
to melt, the men raised dugout canoes from the muddy shallows where they had been sub-
merged to prevent splitting, loaded their families and household gear, and headed for fishing
camps. By mid-March the suckers were running in the Williamson and the Sprague. The
people fished at stone weirs with dip nets, gill net baskets, two-pronged harpoons, and multi-
barbed spears. On the Lost River near Olene there was a famous fishing station where Klamaths and Modocs camped for weeks, catching and drying an estimated fifty tons of fish.

Spring progressed, and the runs of salmon and suckers dwindled. Families set out on the
meadows to dig camas and arrowroot (for which Chewaucan Marsh was named—Fremont
said the marsh looked like it had been plowed when his party of explorers passed through
in the 1850s). They harvested the roots of cattail and tule, wild celery and mosses, gathered
the eggs of swans and other waterbirds, and fished for trout in the mountain streams. Women
used stone-lined ovens to bake camas and other vegetables for winter storage. The families
drew together again in midsummer as pond lily seeds, known as *wokas,* ripened on the
marshes (over 10,000 acres on the Klamath Marsh alone). In fall the men went to hunt an-
telope, mule deer, and mountain sheep in the east. Women, children, and old men went to
the mountains for huckleberries, serviceberries, chokecherries, and wild plums. Waterbirds
were taken by men in canoes hiding among tules, using nets. Beaver, otter, and rabbits were

Mary Gentry, member-at-large
for the Executive Committee
of the Klamath tribes, Klamath
Marsh, Oregon, 1998.

Below: Mule deer,
Horse Mountain,
California.

also netted. By mid-October the people were rebuilding their earth lodges, gathering fire-wood, preparing for another winter. Slow but never simple, the rhythms of their lives gave them, through the demands of survival, an intimacy with the intertwined processes of life in their home territories that is probably unparalleled, and possibly partway lost already. If so, that is an appalling result of their conquest, a loss people in the Klamath Basin will suffer for in the long run, as they try to relearn what the native people already knew.

These were not people who called themselves Klamaths. That name was a white person's invention. Their ancient political affinities were loosely organized, leadership shared by shamans. By 1835 men had gone to the Dalles on the Columbia River to trade for horses and guns. Their culture was becoming more aggressive and materialistic just as settlers be-gan arriving.

Experienced farmers could see that the fertile peat-ground fringes of the great marshes were likely to be a cropland paradise. But as settlers began laying out boundaries, breaking up plow grounds, building houses, there were violent conflicts with the native people. It was clear to them the Indians had to be relocated.

Gadwall,
Miller Lake,
Oregon.

Summer evening,

Miller Lake,

Oregon.

"Conservation is a state of harmony between men and land.

By land is meant all of the things on, over, or in the earth."

While the native people were used to the concept of vaguely defined tribal territories, even the idea that a fishing hole might be the property of an individual or family, they were not used to operating in a system of rules that defined each piece of land and stream flow as belonging specifically to one individual or group of individuals. It wasn't that the native people didn't believe in property. It was just that they didn't believe every one thing was property, or that individual ownership defined what was most essential about things. The tools they carried were owned by a single person; but rather than own specific lands they claimed primary rights to use certain places, and inhabited communally claimed territories. The tribes thought of themselves as sovereign, but believed, according to the testimony of living tribal members, that spiritual aspects of life were vastly more important than property. Which many settlers also believed. But white society didn't often, at least officially, act out that belief.

The problems for settlers were simple. The Indians had to understand what was theirs and what was not; they had to give up their wandering. They had to be nailed into place. They had to be reeducated. Then, around them, after they were enclosed, settlers could farm and run cows and sheep and build roads and railroads and towns. Civilization could proceed.

In matters of the law, at least, what was intended was justice. The ancestors of the people who colonized the Klamath Basin came to America to escape oppression in Europe. However backward native life might have seemed to them, this was the New World. Justice was the essential basis for life. The Indians had to be treated fairly. In endless incidents, of course, they weren't. But that was the official line.

The Indians would have to learn to live on a rigidly boundaried enclave inside the white civilization, but it would be large enough, rich enough in terms of timbered uplands where they could hunt, and marshlands and lakes and streams where they could fish, to allow them to go on living in traditional ways. Indians could wander all they wanted inside their reservation. That was the idea. But boundaries for the reservation weren't easy to define. The Klamaths claimed enormous territories, an ancient domain where they said their people had lived for more than ten thousand years, consisting of more than 20 million acres.

In October 1864, various tribes and the federal government, at Council Grove near the Wood River just north of Fort Klamath, negotiated and signed an agreement reserving 1.18 million acres of resource-rich lands north and east of Klamath Lake for tribal life. Reservation boundaries ran from Crater Butte in the north, Gearhart Mountain to the east, to Pelican Butte, Crater Lake, and Mount Thielsen in the west—"mountaintop to mountaintop." It was territory that since "time immemorial" had been inhabited by people the white culture had decided to collect into the "Klamath Tribe."

Modocs and Paiutes were also located on traditional Klamath lands. Modocs and Klamaths share a common language and an ancient bloodstock. But by the time the white people arrived their relationship was mostly based on trade. Modocs lived in the hills south of the basin and thought of themselves primarily as hunters; Klamaths lived near lakes and swamps and rivers, and they were fisherfolk. The results of shoving Klamaths and Modocs together on a single reservation were before long bloody and tragic.

Mourning doves,
Timber Mountain,
California.

Shield volcano,

Medicine Lake Highland,

California.

A federal agent in California had negotiated an unauthorized treaty with the Modocs, reserving a territory for them south of Tule Lake. Which was where the Modocs wanted to live, on what they thought of as their homeland.

In November 1872, weary of intertribal conflict on the reservation, a man named Kintpuash (Captain Jack) and fifty-two Modoc warriors returned to Tule Lake and occupied the lava beds south of the lake. For six months they held off a thousand U.S. soldiers, among them a company of Oregon Volunteers, and seventy-eight Warm Springs Indian scouts.

The Modoc War, as it was called, cost the federal government nearly a half million dollars and the lives of over four hundred soldiers. The Modoc, conducting guerrilla warfare in the broken grounds of the lava beds, lost thirteen warriors. The United States military establishment, its primary efforts since the end of the Civil War devoted to making the West safe for settlement and economic development, was frustrated and humiliated. Settlers who had staked their futures in the Klamath Basin were frightened and angered. Their society, people who thought of themselves as hardworking, honest, decent, and fair-minded, was officially infuriated.

In April 1873, General Edward Canby, the ranking military officer, began negotiations with the Modocs in an effort to get them to return to the Klamath Reservation. Captain Jack and his men ambushed the negotiators, killing Canby and two others. The army redoubled its efforts, and on June 1, 1873, Captain Jack surrendered to the United States Army.

On October 3, 1873, Captain Jack, Schonchen John, Black Jim, and Boston Charlie were hanged at Fort Klamath for the murder of Canby and the others. Captain Jack's body was dug up, pumped full of formaldehyde, and shown in carnivals along the East Coast. Two Modoc warriors were sent to the Alcatraz Island military prison in San Francisco Bay, and 153 Modocs were sent to Fort Quapaw, Oklahoma. A generation later their descendants were allowed (if they wanted) to return to the Klamath Reservation.

The most spectacular problem involved in relocating the Klamath Basin Indians was considered, after these measures, to be solved. But the difficulties brought on by relocating native peoples were just beginning.

In 1871 the Klamath tribes complained that the reservation boundary didn't honor the intended dimensions of their entitlement, as laid down in the Treaty of 1864, "from mountaintop to mountaintop." A survey confirmed that 624,000 acres had been left out of the reservation. The Klamath tribes were paid about 85 cents per acre for this land (nothing for the timber).

It was intended that reservation lands would not be encroached upon, but there was still considerable unauthorized settlement by whites. The General Allotment Act of 1887 (which awarded tribal members specific landholdings) was meant to encourage tribal people to farm and ranch. But most of the allotted acreage was not suitable for crops or large enough to support grazing. And since allotments could be sold, tribal lands were open to white settlement. Only by buying up a number of allotments were ranchers with a line of credit or capital (mostly white, my grandfather among them) able to amass enough acres to support a functional cattle operation.

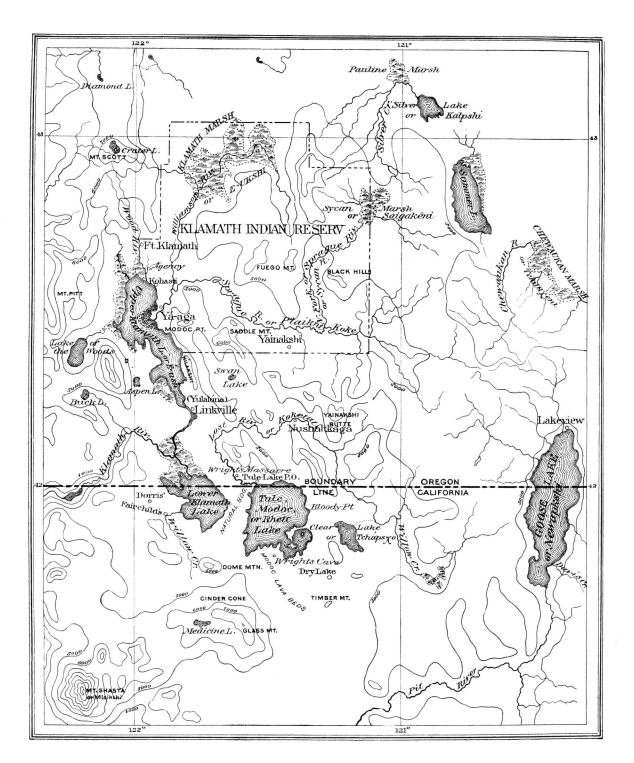

Historical map of the Klamath Basin, including the Klamath Reservation. From Albert Samuel Gatschet, *The Klamath Indians of Southwestern Oregon* (Washington, D.C.: Government Printing Office, 1890).

Two hundred and fifty thousand acres passed from tribal control. (In 1937 a court-of-claims decision awarded the Klamath tribes more than $7 million for these losses. Twenty-seven percent of those monies was deducted to cover federal support of the Klamath tribes since the Treaty of 1864.)

In 1913 Klamath tribal members began receiving per capita payments for tribal timber sold on their behalf by the Bureau of Indian Affairs. In 1954 they owned more ponderosa pine than anybody else in the West, 4.6 billion board feet, 1.5 billion of that in untouched stands. Tribal members were obviously aware that their holdings were of enormous value. Many believed the Bureau of Indian Affairs was selling their timber to logging and milling corporations at less than market value.

In the late 1940s Senator Arthur Watkins of Utah began advocating reservation termination, or as he called it, "on the spot freedom," saying the Klamaths were "ready." But the Klamath people, while deeply interested in greater control over their own future and resources, never wanted to sell their reservation. In 1948 the Klamath superintendent, Raymond Bitney, wrote the Indian Affairs commissioner, saying that "the General Council of the Klamath Tribe has consistently opposed any attempts to liquidate the Klamath Reservation." The tribe never agreed to the Klamath Termination Act, Public Law 587, which was passed in August of 1954. The closest they came was when in January 1954 the General Council authorized "conditional acceptance" of "eventual termination."

John Collier, commissioner of Indian Affairs from 1932 until 1945, wrote in 1957 that conditional consent was "wrung from the tribal members through what must be called extortion." Most of the tribe was living in poverty, and $2.6 million in tribal money was being withheld by the Joint Subcommittee on Indian Affairs pending tribal agreement to termination.

(There is another, unverifiable story—that the Klamath tribes planned to cut their own timber and haul it to a tribally owned lumber mill that would be built at Chiloquin, where they would process their own timber. The tribe could have no doubt found the capital. But agents from the Bureau of Indian Affairs and major timber corporations would have been cut off. The mill-town economy of Klamath Falls would have suffered.)

These events took place before the Indian Civil Rights Act of 1968 (Public Law 90-284), which required tribal consent on such matters. At no time did the Klamath people agree to, or were they even given a chance to, vote on termination. The Congress of the United States, on August 13, 1954, with what John Collier called the "nominal consent" of two representatives of the tribe, passed the Klamath Termination Act.

On the final tribal roll there were 2,133 individuals. Of these, 1,660 elected to withdraw from the tribe and take their interests in cash. The remaining 473 retained their interests in land. A proportionate part of the tribal land was transferred to a private trustee to administer for them. The rest of the land was sold to pay withdrawing tribal members. Some 70 percent of that property was purchased by the U.S. Fish and Wildlife Service or the Winema National Forest.

It should be emphasized that these decisions on the part of Klamath tribal members—take the money or not—were made after the issue of termination was settled, by people who had not voted to terminate. The results were disastrous. Exploitation of Indian people by Klamath Basin businesspeople and lawyers was notorious.

In the next decades 40 percent of all deaths among the Klamath people were alcohol caused or related; 52 percent of the deaths within the tribe occurred among people under forty; infant mortality rates were twice that of the general population; and 70 percent of the Klamaths dropped out before graduating from high school. Indian poverty levels in Klamath County were three times those of non-Indians. In 1977 the Klamath Alcohol and Drug Abuse Council estimated that 77 percent of all Indian deaths were alcohol or drug related.

But as Elwood Miller Jr., the director of natural resources for the Klamath tribe, told me, things are better now: "We live in our homeland, and the world can restore itself."

Conservationist agendas and those of many Indian people have come to more and more frequently coincide. This conjunction of interests is beginning to be of enormous economic importance in the Klamath Basin. Outsiders, backed by ecological scientists, by conservation and environmental laws, and by courts that insist on enforcement of tribal rights belonging to Native American groups, are going to be defining an increasing number of policies in the Klamath Basin.

Summer storm,

Klamath Marsh,

Oregon.

5

EARTHWORKS

When I was a child visiting on Jefferson Street in Klamath Falls with my mother's parents, in a house since torn down and replaced by a parking lot, I was warned, "Don't play near the canal!"

The canal, flowing thick with green water or mysteriously dry, the banks hung with dead weeds, cut across the low end of Jefferson Street and looped around the football field at Klamath Union High School. I had no sense of what purpose it served, where it came from or went, nor of the expense of spirit and labor its creation had involved. It did not seem, to a boy, like one of the works of man. It seemed like part of nature.

During the settlement of the Klamath Basin, the economy was centered on grazing and livestock. Ranchers cut and stacked hay off natural streamside and lakeshore meadowlands. But it was evident there wasn't enough to go around. Ironically, in a place so abundantly watered, rainfall was insufficient for raising hay (or for cropland farming). The Klamath Basin was, after all, part of the arid West. The necessary thing, since it would support ranches and possibly farming, was irrigation.

The town of Linkville was founded in 1867 by George Nurse and Edgar Overton alongside the Link River between Klamath Lake and Lake Ewauna. It was a natural town site, high ground by the river looking out to the south and Mount Shasta. Hot water bubbling from springs was used for heating (and still is).

In 1868 the Langell family settled beside the Lost River (so named because of the way its waters spread and the channel was lost in the meadowlands). Through rechanneling they reclaimed 4,000 acres in Langell Valley for farming and ranching. In the 1870s James Poe did the same thing ten miles downstream in Poe Valley. In 1878 a ditch was begun at a headgate in the Link River, where it flows from Klamath Lake, to run water through the city for use by the owners of town lots. In 1884 that ditch was extended into the sagebrush country east of town. By 1888, known as the Ankeny-Henley Canal it ran eight miles southeast, split into easterly and southerly branches, and irrigated four thousand acres. In the sum-

mer of 1882, the Van Brimmer brothers began construction of a ditch to supply water for 4,000 acres lying on the south and west sides of the Lost River near Merrill. In 1886 J. Frank Adams completed a six-mile ditch from the Lost River to Adams Point. By 1904 it ran twenty-two miles around the north side of Tule Lake. Work on these projects was done with teams, hand-operated Fresno scrapers, picks and shovels, with sweat and broken fingers, and dreams.

High hopes seemed justified. Barley near Keno yielded an "astonishing" 36 bushels per acre. In 1892 a farmer reported that "crops can be produced with less effort than any place on the coast and perhaps in the known world." Obed Short, the first basin "potato king," started raising spuds in 1894. A decade later he planted 80 acres south of Klamath Falls and harvested up to 350 bushels per acre. All he had to do, he said, was "plant, harrow, and harvest."

As the century turned, Congress finally acted on John Wesley Powell's vision. Their purpose was to induce settlement. Francis Newlands was a senator from Nevada who'd left for the East, made his fortune practicing law, married a Comstock mining heiress, and come back West with ruling-class powers. In 1888 he financed the Truckee Irrigation Project, and lost $500,000 and his taste for private reclamation projects.

Newlands's chance to promote public water development came in 1901, when William McKinley was assassinated and Theodore Roosevelt became president. Teddy was infatuated with the West and convinced that John Wesley Powell had been correct about the need for coherent western water development. Failure to fully utilize western rivers, Roosevelt said, was a national disgrace. Roosevelt's chief ally in Congress was Senator Newlands, who pro-

posed "nationalizing the works of irrigation." But this sounded like socialism. Roosevelt took charge, restated the idea in acceptable terms, and on June 17, 1902, the National Reclamation Act (also known as the Newlands Act) became law, creating the United States Reclamation Service.

Lands in the projects funded by the Reclamation Service were to be sold to individuals in parcels not to exceed 80 acres, for amounts contingent on development costs. The lands would be paid for in ten annual installments. A revolving fund, with no other purpose than reclamation, would soon materialize. That was the original plan. Not surprisingly, the first project authorized was on the Carson and Truckee Rivers of Nevada, in Senator Newlands's backyard. The draining down of Pyramid Lake and the loss to near extinction of its landlocked cutthroat trout are among the results. So is the creation of farmlands around Fallon and the enfranchised, productive lives of farmers there, over generations.

Within three years huge projects were authorized on the Salt River in Arizona, on the Platte in Nebraska, on the Shoshone in Wyoming, on the Milk River in Montana, on the Strawberry in Utah, on the Rio Grande in New Mexico, on the Uncompahgre in Colorado, and on the Umatilla and Klamath in Oregon.

Marshlands provided wild hay to settlers with horse-drawn mowers. Photograph by Maud Baldwin. Courtesy of The Klamath County Museum.

DIGGING "SPUDS" ON ALTAMONT RANCH.   DUNCAN 115

In October 1903, an engineer from the Reclamation Service made a preliminary horseback tour of the Klamath Basin and estimated that various storage possibilities could ensure the irrigation of 200,000 acres of agricultural land.

In November 1904, Frederick H. Newell, head of the Reclamation Service, addressed a group of farmers in Klamath Falls. Newell said they were living in a perfect irrigation project, and that he was sure the secretary of interior would authorize construction, given four conditions:

1. All conflicting and vested water rights had to be adjudicated.
2. All riparian rights on Lower Klamath and Tule Lakes had to be surrendered.
3. Oregon and California had to cede to the federal government all rights and title to Lower Klamath and Tule Lakes and enact laws that would permit lowering or raising the lakes' waters.
4. The United States Congress had to give the secretary of interior the power to destroy navigability on those lakes.

Nobody locally or in the Reclamation Service seems to have thought about the Indians and their prior rights to all the waters necessary to maintain their way of life. It was to be a fateful oversight.

By February 1905, conditions had been met, and the Klamath Project was approved by Congress. Tule Lake and Lower Klamath Lake were to be "dewatered" by diversion and evaporation. Plans called for (1) constructing the Clear Lake and Gerber Dams to impound floodwaters; (2) diverting the Lost River when not needed, by means of a diversion dam on Lost River and a canal to the Klamath River; and (3) taking water from Upper Klamath Lake, through headworks, into what would eventually become an elaborate basinwide irrigation system.

Work on extending existing canals was begun in 1906; construction of the Clear Lake Dam took place in 1909 and 1910; the Lost River Diversion Dam was finished in 1912; Gerber Dam was constructed in 1924 and 1925. All of these projects facilitated both "dewatering" and irrigation.

But a recital of dates and facts misses the heart of this story, which has to do with promises and dreams, with hard work and the rewards earned by such effort and diligence. Heavy snowfall, hard rains, and the need to haul equipment forty miles over mountains held up canal work in the spring of 1906. During blasting, horses were scalded by water from hot springs and had to be killed. Teams of horses dislodged boulders with chains, and derricks raised them. Men with wheelbarrows moved the smaller rocks. Finished canals, built across gravelly hills and marshy peat-soil flats, often leaked and were lined with red fir planks and relined with concrete.

Austrians, Montenegrins, and Serbians made up much of the workforce on the Clear Lake Dam. They excavated under the dam site to bedrock, basalt slabs with seams of porous lava. The seams were dug out and filled with concrete. The trench was refilled with four-inch layers of rock and earth, which were compacted by a four-ton cast-iron roller, layer after layer until the dam was completed—42 feet high and 840 feet along its crest—in 1910. All this, toward realization of an enfranchising dream, with teams of horses and steam pumps and manpower.

Western irrigation development was from the beginning understood as answering a public responsibility. Without federal irrigation the West was going to become depopulated. Settlers were giving up, heading back for the East. Marc Reisner, in *Cadillac Desert,* writes, "To block a federal reclamation project was to block all further migration to the West and to ensure disaster for those who were already there—or for those who were on their way."

Passage of the Reclamation Act was called a triumph for the common person. But while limits to landownership were in the law, they were not rigorously enforced. The Reclamation Service didn't actively confront the problem of ownership that exceeded those limitations. The Salt River Project near Phoenix, in 1946, more than fifty years after it was authorized, was still being farmed by 134 "noncomplying" owners, who together held more than 30,000 acres, over 12 percent of the irrigated land inside the project. Engineers in Reclamation were devoted to building beautiful dams, remaking landforms into works of art (parts of which often resembled depopulated nightmares by Magritte and de Chirico). Engineers, as has been true in the history of public works from Assyria to the Atomic Energy Commission, were not concerned about creating yeoman democracies. Nor did Reclamation pursue the repayment program with any particular vigor. By 1922, only 10 percent of funds loaned to settlers on projects had been repaid, and 60 percent of the irrigators were defaulting on repayment. The Reclamation Fund was close to nonexistent. According to Donald Worster, the people who ran the Reclamation Service were "overwhelmingly an elite group promoting an elite program. Their overriding aim was to enlarge, for their own ends, the country's wealth and influence." Short-term results, irrigated acres, were the prime objective. Long-term ecological problems like salinization and pollution from chemical fertilizers and pesticides, and social problems like the need for curbing use of public money to further enhance the fortunes of the privileged, were left for the future to deal with.

Mallards,
Williamson River
delta, Oregon.

Frozen forest,

Mount Thielsen,

Cascade Range,

Oregon.

Winter, Sycan Marsh,
Oregon.

Long Creek, Oregon.

Greater white-fronted geese,
Upper Klamath Lake,
Oregon.

Badgers, Klamath Marsh,
Oregon.

Blacktailed jackrabbit,
Clear Lake Hills,
California.

Rock wren,
Sagebrush Butte,
California.

Prairie falcon,
The Peninsula,
California.

Northern harrier,

Klamath Marsh,

Oregon.

Summer,
Sycan Marsh,
Oregon.

Western watershed
boundary, Mount Thielsen,
Cascade Range, Oregon.

American marten,
Walker Rim,
Oregon.

Ross' geese,
Williamson River delta,
Oregon.

Eared grebe,
Lower Klamath
Lake, California.

FEATHERS

Carleton Watkins photographed sea lions and pelagic birds on the Farallon Islands in the 1870s. Eadweard Muybridge in 1877 caught animals on the move for his book *Animal Locomotion,* using shutter speeds of one-thousandth of a second. The telephoto lens was patented in 1891, and wide-angle lenses were available by 1900. Wildlife conservation work in the United States got wind in its sail at the same time the art of wildlife photography was being perfected. The conjunction isn't entirely an accident. Wildlife photographs, widely circulated, obviously stimulated an interest in the fates of animals themselves.

Citizens who came to America with the objective of liberating themselves from the constraints of life in Europe and Asia, seeking liberty and opportunity, were often beguiled to the point of reverence by the thronging glories they encountered.

As wildlife photography began to be reproduced in books and magazines, a wide population of middle-class people, many in cities, while distant from "nature" could revere it from afar. In 1876 George Bird Grinnell of Yale became editor of *Forest and Stream* magazine. In 1887 Grinnell called for the formation of a society dedicated to the protection of nongame species of birds. He named his group the Audubon Society. Nearly forty thousand people joined in the first year.

In the 1890s, in Portland, Oregon, William Finley was a boy obsessed with birds. He made friends with a neighbor boy, Herman Bohlman. They collected bird skins and eggs, sold them to collectors, and became noted for their ability to track down rare specimens. By 1899 they had turned to ornithological photography. In 1901 a National Association of Audubon Societies was formed. In 1902 an Oregon chapter was organized, largely due to the efforts of William Finley.

Finley and Bohlman started going off every summer on expeditions. In 1901 and 1903 they went to Three Arches Rocks on the Oregon coast near Tillamook Bay to photograph seabirds. At Three Arches Rocks on Sundays, boats filled with "sport hunters" would locate under the cliffs so gunners could fire into nesting bird colonies. Beaches were littered with dead, rotting birds. In 1904, in great part through Finley's efforts, an Oregon Model Bird Law put an end to the festivities.

Finley's next objective, shutting down the plume-hunting trade, the killing of birds in order to gather feathers for women's hats, took longer to realize. On Lower Klamath Lake the plume hunters found their "most profitable field in the West." Grebes, terns, and gulls by the thousands were slaughtered, their skins shipped to New York in bales for use by milliners. Mature birds were killed; eggs were left to rot in the nests, the young to starve. In 1904 the National Association of Audubon Societies, on the advice of Finley, paid for wardens to enforce the Oregon Model Bird Law in the Klamath Basin. Finley was an informant against a Portland millinery firm that sold egret plumes.

After spending the summer of 1904 in California photographing great blue herons and golden eagles, Finley and Bohlman went to visit the marshlands in the Lower Klamath Basin in 1905. Lower Klamath Lake and Tule Lake were surrounded by a "jungle" of tules in an "impenetrable mass from ten to fifteen feet high." Colonies of nesting birds clustered on an "endless area of floating tule islands" composed of decaying generations of vegetation

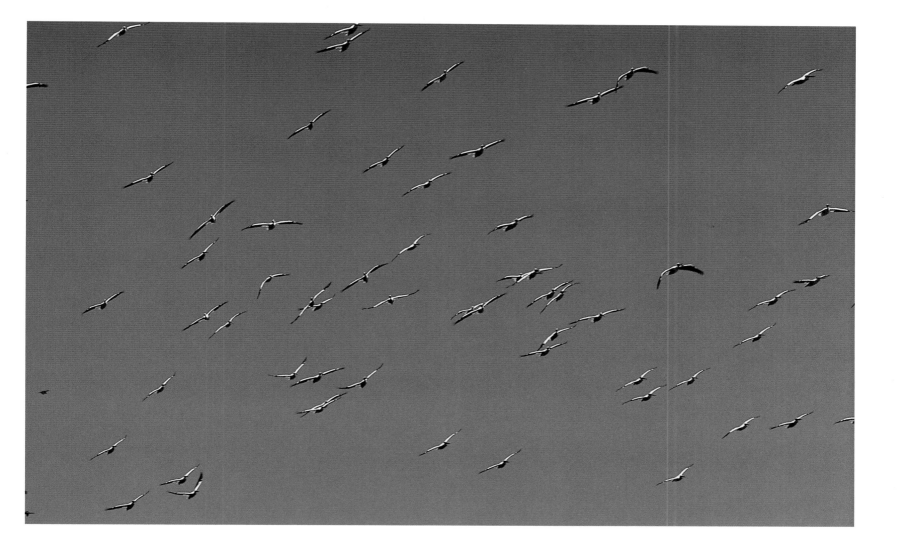

with green shoots sprouting from underneath. Walking on those floating islands, Finley said, was like walking on snow drifts. You never knew if you would break through. The islands held white pelican rookeries, each with 400 to 600 birds. The total number was estimated at more than 4,000, possibly as many as 9,000, one of the largest breeding colonies of pelicans anywhere. It was, Finley said, "perhaps the greatest feeding and breeding ground for waterfowl on the Pacific coast" and "perhaps the most extensive breeding ground in the West for all kinds of inland water birds." There were colonies of gulls, terns, and grebes, but plume hunters had killed out the heron rookeries. Each winter, camps of professional hunters were still killing enormous numbers of ducks and geese, "game birds," for the San Francisco restaurant trade. Finley said that "when the birds are flying, each hunter will bag from one hundred to one hundred fifty birds a day." One hundred and twenty tons of ducks were shipped to San Francisco during the winter of 1903.

Finley published stories and photographs of the bird life in the Lower Klamath Marsh,

American white pelicans,
Tule Lake, California.

Market hunters pose on the deck of a steamboat, circa 1911. Photograph by Miller Photo Company. Courtesy of The Klamath County Museum.

exposing in national magazines the disgrace that was unlimited market hunting and emphasizing the need for wildlife habitat protection. "A very large number of lakes and ponds have been drained and swamps have been dried up under the guise of making agricultural land," he wrote, and "remaining lakes, ponds, and swamps must be preserved." Or, he finished, "many species are sure to be pushed to the point of final disappearance."

Citizens, informed by writers and photographers like Finley, began to understand that industrial harvesting of natural resources might ruin nature as habitat for the intensely complex interwoven system of life-forms human beings had evolved to live within. It was possible to foresee a denuded earth. People saw a need to insist on preserving so-called pristine nature. Many were educated, economically privileged, and politically powerful. The environmental movement was being born.

Conservationists and naturalists, like irrigators, found an ally in Teddy Roosevelt. George Bird Grinnell persuaded Roosevelt to create the nation's first national wildlife refuge, at Pelican Island, Florida, in 1903. In 1907, after seeing the photographs taken by Finley and Bohlman at Three Arches Rocks, Roosevelt declared it the first bird refuge on the West

Coast. In 1908, largely as a result of Finley's efforts, Roosevelt created the Lower Klamath Lake and the Malheur Lake National Wildlife Refuges in Oregon to preserve nesting grounds for migratory waterfowl. These were the largest wildlife refuges that had been authorized. They were the first on land of agricultural value.

Lower Klamath was also the first wildlife refuge established in a watershed being revamped by the Reclamation Service. The conflicts inherent in establishing a wildlife refuge inside a reclamation district would have to be worked out on the ground. Finley wrote, "We move to conserve or develop one resource while at the same time, we are destroying another." In 1911 the Clear Lake National Wildlife Refuge was established by executive order of President William Howard Taft. At that same time, Reclamation botanists decided that soils in the Lower Klamath Basin were too alkaline for crops. They could find no economically sensible method to remove the alkali. Plans for draining the lake were postponed. This was bad news for local developers, who had claimed 20,000 acres in Lower Klamath under the Swamp Land Act.

Despite warnings that peat soils could catch fire and burn interminably if drained before

Long-billed curlew,
Lower Klamath Lake,
California.

an irrigation system was in place, the president of the Klamath Water Users Association spent months in Washington, D.C., lobbying to have Lower Klamath removed from the federal reclamation project so landowners could dike the private lands and pump off the water. In 1915 an executive order from President Woodrow Wilson reduced the Lower Klamath Lake National Wildlife Refuge from 80,000 acres to 53,600 acres in order to facilitate the conversion of additional wetlands to agriculture.

With the help of the Reclamation Service employees, a Lower Klamath Lake drainage district was organized. Headgates through a railway embankment were closed in 1917, shutting off water from the Klamath River. By the summer of 1918 the marshes were dry. Mudflats extended into the lake. Some 85,000 acres were dried up. By 1922 all that remained was a 365-acre pond.

Thousands of ducks died of alkali poisoning. Nesting colonies of gulls, cormorants, and pelicans vanished. Fire broke out in the peat soils. Clouds of ash and dust obscured the sun in Klamath Falls. Farming, as had been predicted because of the alkaline soils, was a complete failure. The chief of the United States Biological Survey said, "What was formerly a great wildlife refuge became a desert." In 1925 William Finley wrote that Lower Klamath was "a great desert waste of dry peat and alkali. Over large stretches fire has burned the peat to a depth of one to three feet, leaving a layer of white loose ashes into which one sinks above his knees." In 1927 the president of the National Audubon Society visited Lower Klamath and reported, "I only saw weeds—miles and miles of thickly growing weeds[;] . . . whirlwinds chased each other like ghosts of the wildlife that had departed."

In 1928 the Tule Lake National Wildlife Refuge was established by President Calvin Coolidge as "a refuge and breeding ground for birds." The Lower Klamath refuge, dusty and barren through the 1930s, was a wasteland and a monument, symbolic and actual, to heedlessness and greed. So it seemed, through the dark years of the Great Depression—a dead land that had not so long ago thronged with life, a monument to dreams confounded.

But success in settling the difficult lands of the American West hadn't been managed by people given to quitting. That which had been ruined by developers could be repaired by engineers. J. R. Iakish, an engineer for Reclamation, saw the complex workings of the ir-rigation system very clearly. Runoff water from reclaimed Tule Lake farmlands was being pumped into headwater ditches and reused for irrigation before collecting in the Tule Lake sump, where it was left to evaporate. This was efficient use of the water, but an interrelated set of problems was developing. First, farmers wanted the sump lands for agriculture. Sec-ond, as farmers increased their use of water, the sump would overfill. Third, U.S. Fish and Wildlife Service officials were protesting that not enough freshwater was flowing into the Tule Lake sump. As a consequence, botulism was taking a heavy toll on migratory water-fowl, threatening the population of the Pacific Flyway. And of course there was the Lower Klamath disaster.

The sump in the Tule Lake Basin was overflowing with runoff water, while Lower Klam-ath, only a couple of miles to the west over Sheepy Ridge, was afire, raging with dust storms, and bone dry. Iakish saw that these problems could be subject to a single elegant solution. He proposed constructing a six-thousand-foot tunnel under Sheepy Ridge. Excess water from the Tule Lake sump could be pumped up sixty feet and delivered through the tunnel into Lower Klamath. Problems with wildlife and agriculture could be simultaneously solved.

The tunnel, lined with concrete, was finished on May 25, 1941. The pumping plant was finished in May 1942. Waters flowed through the tunnel, the Lower Klamath wetlands be-gan to refill, and the tules grew, the waterfowl marshes were restored, and the birds began coming back. And, after decades of privately financed development on land abandoned as worthless by the United States Bureau of Reclamation, farmers learned to leach the alkali away in deep drains. Lower Klamath, it turned out, could be farmed, and very profitably. The health of the system was being restored through a series of technological solutions.

By the fall of 1955, refuge counts in Lower Klamath and Tule Lake peaked at upwards of 7 million birds. In a 1956 report the U.S. Fish and Wildlife Service said the Klamath Basin carried "the greatest concentration of waterfowl in North America and probably the world." The watershed could be reconstructed, for human use, without killing off the natural life that had lived there for millennia. That was the clear message.

Snow geese and cackling
Canada geese, Tule Lake,
California.

7

THE REWARDS OF TENACITY

In 1894 Nathan Merrill started developing a town site north of the Lost River. In 1909 a party of Czechs, sixty-five members of the Bohemian Colonization Club from Omaha, settled in the vicinity of the little town of Malin, a few miles east of Merrill. Agnes Drazil remembered those first years: "I was afraid of the new country we came to. I would have gone home but there was no money. It was all in the land. I couldn't ask for things I needed in the grocery store. I didn't know the words; but I knew how to work. I helped grub sage-brush and later helped to harvest the crops. I had nine children, and when I came in from the fields I didn't know what to do first, milk the cow or feed my family or clean the house."

In 1911 Merrill burned. During rebuilding, barges were still able to ferry materials across Tule Lake and up the Lost River to community docks. Nowadays, remnants of the lake lie in sumps a dozen miles to the south.

In May 1916 the director of Reclamation authorized opening 4,000 acres at the north end of the Tule Lake project, south of Merrill and Malin. Each homestead would be 80 acres, and $21,000 would be spent to level the land and install the irrigation system. Ten years' work reclaiming cropland from the waters of Tule Lake was finally paying off.

In April 1917 about 3,000 acres south of the little towns of Merrill and Malin, or thirty-five homestead units, were available. Nearly 180 citizens applied. The applicants included lawyers and bankers, dentists, farmers, and 15 single women. A drawing was held. Twenty-seven units went to locals. Most of them were single men. There were no roads, no indoor plumbing, no running water, no refrigeration, electricity, or telephones. Settlers built shacks. Mud in winter was ankle deep. In summer, dust storms blew up. Water from the shallow wells stank of methane.

In 1920 Merrill burned again. The opera house, the pool hall, and the best restaurant in town were destroyed. In 1921 the town burned again. Fire started in a candy store and burned the meat market, a barber shop, a pharmacy, city hall, and the firehouse. Each time, without hesitation, settlers rebuilt.

The second allotment of settlement units near Tule Lake came in 1922, after the end of World War I. Available farm units numbered 174. But, for a number of reasons, demand was slug-

Donald Rajnus,
potato farmer and
descendant of Czech
settlers, Malin,
Oregon, 1988.

gish. Development fees had been doubled, to $90 per acre. For an 80-acre farm the total was $7,200, to be repaid over twenty years. This, with equipment costs, home building, and the uncertainties of farming on land with no crop history, was seen as too much of a burden. And there had been failures. Only 54 units were awarded.

But by 1923 Malin had a newspaper. And, after failures with exotics like melons, sugar beets, celery, carrots, and strawberries, farmers were making money off staple crops like alfalfa, flax, Hannchen barley, clover, and potatoes.

In January 1927, 145 units were advertised, more than 8,000 acres, with the construction fee cut in half, to $45 per acre. There were schools and barn dances. A community of survivors was making its start. All the homesteads were filed on. In 1930 Vaclav Kalina built a theater in Malin to accommodate talking movies. But the roads were still so bad people drove along the railroad tracks in rainy seasons.

In 1928 the Tule Lake Community Club formed, with the objective of getting schools built on the California side of the project, as well as bridges and roads. They lobbied, and homesteaders were appointed to the Project Selection Board. In 1929 they persuaded Reclamation to announce that a "Government Town Site" would be established three miles south of the California border, beside the Southern Pacific railroad tracks. Two hundred and nine city lots were offered at public auction in 1931. Tulelake was born, a Wild West farmer boomtown. Soon there was a legendary string of bars thronging with migrant farmhands and hell-raising, on-the-town bird hunters.

A cascade of rabbit ears was
the result of an organized
rabbit drive by homesteaders.
Courtesy of The Klamath
County Museum.

In 1935, when I was a child, we lived on the second floor of a stone building on Broadway in Malin. My father raised turkeys, hauling them out on a flatbed truck in crates, dumping them to pick in farm fields, then reloading in the evening. Just before Thanksgiving the turkeys were slaughtered in a railway car on a siding at Tulelake. I remember a party in Malin, my mother dancing with my father. They were young, and they were in love, or so I imagine, and I sorrow for my loss of them.

When I was going to high school in Klamath Falls in the 1940s, we thought the sky was the limit once you got across the California line and found yourself on the mean streets of Tulelake. Boys could buy beer anywhere.

Vaclav Kalina brought "big bands," Harry James and the Dorsey Brothers, to Malin in the 1930s. Ager's Cafe in Tulelake was described as "the Wall Street of western barley, the crying wall of the potato industry."

The Great Depression, with its desperate Okies and Arkies and CCC Camps, and then World War II, with the Japanese Internment Camp at Newell (south of Tulelake), came

KLAMATH HUNTERS   H 70

and went. Homestead children grew up, married, and the land passed to the next generation. Homestead families, who got started hanging on any way they could, grew prosperous, built white houses alongside paved roads, and planted orchards.

By 1946 it had been ten years since a homestead allotment. The Bureau of Reclamation
delayed proceedings so World War II veterans would have a chance to file. On December
18, a drawing was held in the Klamath Falls armory. The ceremonies played on the radio
all up and down the West Coast. There were eighty-six winners. Their names were picked
from a pickle jar filled with 1,305 gelatin capsules, each containing a slip of paper with a
number. The Klamath Union High School band played as the capsules were picked from
the jar one by one, broken open with a wooden mallet, the numbers read, a list consulted.
Winners cried and laughed. Some got drunk, others prayed. Speeches were given. The nation, listening in, was proud of itself. Moments like this validated a lot of struggle. No more
Great Depression, no more war. Gerald Corcoran, a new settler, said, "All it takes is a little
cooperation and we can get the crops in and get our houses fixed up and everything going
fine by the end of the year." This was the perfect American story, the dream realized. Independence and prosperity were only a ration of work and sweat away. John Wesley Powell would have been happy to think his vision of yeoman democracy in the irrigation West
was actual.

But the Bureau of Reclamation and the U.S. Fish and Wildlife Service were always loom-
ing in the background. This land, in so many ways, was also their land.

In 1948, when 2,300 acres at the southern end of the Tule Lake refuge were opened for homesteading, conservationists and sport hunters threw a fit. Henry Clineschmidt, head of the Associated Sportsmen of California, wrote, "This lake has been squeezed down from 25,000 acres 20 years ago to only 16,500 acres[, and] . . . they are continuing to drain the lake as fast as they can, pumping it into the Lower Klamath Basin whenever rain swells the lake threatening the Holland-like dykes. However, when fresh water is urgently needed to halt an epidemic of botulism killing thousands of ducks in the lower lake area, no water is being pumped. . . . It is such systematic waste as this as [sic] will, in the not too distant future, toll the death knell to the West's greatest refuge." Farmers countered that their fields were devastated by thousands of feeding ducks and geese, and that hunters were constantly tromping planted ground.

The last homestead drawing was held on February 15, 1949, in the Tulelake American Legion Hall. Ernest Lee Thacker of Hemet, California, accepted 137 acres of alkaline soil south of Malin, the least desirable unit in the drawing. No one knew it at the time, but he was the last homesteader in the Tule Lake Basin.

Around 22,000 acres in the Tule Lake National Wildlife Refuge were not released for homesteading, but were leased to farmers. The official justification for the lease-land program, as stated in a recent U.S. Fish and Wildlife Service Environmental Assessment, is that it "aided in developing the land during the construction of irrigation and drainage facilities to serve farm units and permit homestead entry." No doubt pressure from local farmers was a prime reason the lease-land program was initiated. The finest soils in the basin were not being farmed. No matter that they belonged to a wildlife refuge; it was a bad thing and should not be allowed. Good land should be farmed. It was a moral as well as economic issue. It can be imagined that the U.S. Fish and Wildlife Service simply rolled over in the face of local pressure. Farming on the lease lands was a way of encouraging proven farmers and cooperating with the local economic interests. The result was a scramble to farm as much of the lease land as possible. The farmer who got a berm plowed around one of the 100-acre lease-land plots got the lease. High-speed plow tractors ran day and night. Nobody in the offices at Reclamation had the guts to kick them off. Family fortunes were made. That's the legend. A grocery store in Tulelake stayed open long after dark for itinerant field hands; a fleet of combines harvested a sick neighbor's barley crop on a single afternoon. That's the other side of the legend.

But conflict over the allocation of the lease lands—the League of Nations and the Frog Pond, lands leased by Tulana Farms (U.S. Fish and Wildlife Service lands developed for farming by the Bureau of Reclamation)—was just beginning. Hunters and conservationists wanted the land reflooded and turned back into wildlife marshes. Farmers wanted the lease lands sold into private ownership. In 1954 Douglas McKay, former governor of Oregon, became secretary of interior. Klamath Basin farmers sent him a brief that said, "We do not believe it is to the best interests of our country and its great system of free enterprise to turn over large tracts of land to federal agencies for permanent ownership and management." McKay disappointed them. My father described him as a "turncoat." The lease lands were not sold to private owners, and the federal government didn't act on the issue for another decade.

In 1964 the California senator Thomas Kuchel successfully proposed legislation that said the refuges in the Klamath Basin "shall be administered by the Secretary of Interior for the major purpose of waterfowl management, but with full consideration to optimum agricultural use that is consistent herewith." It was at best a vaguely stated mandate, but certain things were obvious. There would be no homesteading on refuge lands, and agriculture would be allowed on refuge lease lands only if farming practices were consistent with wildlife management. All available lands in the Klamath irrigation project were being farmed. Divvying up would go on indefinitely, but there wouldn't be any more. Seen at the time as a victory for the U.S. Fish and Wildlife Service, the Kuchel Act has been subject to self-interested interpretation by all sides ever since its passage.

The issue of who was in control of lease lands, the Bureau of Reclamation or the U.S. Fish and Wildlife Service, was seemingly resolved in August 1977, when the Fish and Wildlife Service refused primary responsibility for managing farmed lands on the refuges and entered into a cooperative agreement that gave Reclamation clear mandate to manage those lands and water flowing to and from them. Reasons for this agreement were obvious. Someone had to be in charge, and Reclamation was better equipped for it. It was called a practical decision. But the consequences of placing the management of refuge lands and water in the hands of an agency designed to serve farmers rather than wildlife have been mixed at best. Farmers expect Reclamation to serve agricultural interests. After all, farmers are trying to make a living. And feed everybody. And support the local economy.

Conservationists say it's obvious that Reclamation, through the cooperative agreement, has not always served the best interests of the wildlife refuges. They say Reclamation objectives and the Kuchel Act ought to be rethought, and soon.

The streets of Tulelake are quiet these days. The population is down to about a third of what it was in the 1940s. People trade in Klamath Falls. It's a common thing, small towns dying. Blame it on paved roads, telephones, and farmers doing business by fax and e-mail. Old-timers move out to spend their last years on a seacoast. Deals and combines and people running them move faster. Properties are consolidated. Communities, and their inherent intimacies, begin to wither.

The rightly lamented shrinking of small towns is the result of fundamental changes in the ways farmers and ranchers go about their business. Blame it on scale, the size of things, mechanization, and the industrialization of work. Farming is very different than it was in the 1920s, when workers picked up spuds from fields by hand, sack by sack. Now potatoes are dug and gathered and dumped into trucks and hauled to storage in long cellars without ever being touched. Irrigation these days is not often just a man with his #2 shovel, out flooding his field. It involves enormously expensive wheel-line and solid-set Rain Bird sprinklers. Tractors and combines come equipped with cabs and heaters, radios, power steering, and air-conditioning. Such changes were intended to make farming and livestock raising more efficient, less driven by the inexorable demands of field labor. Farmers smile and say, "I get to go fishing once in a while."

But an unintended result of mechanization has been loss of neighbor-to-neighbor connection and more emphasis on economic efficiency rather than agricultural artistry. On

Human-killed coyote, Double
Head Lake, California.

profits rather than long-term husbandry. Combines and pesticides cost a lot of money. Farmers are often irrevocably tied to bankers, and to the equipment dealers who provide them
with the combines, and to the chemical companies that sell them fertilizers and pesticides.
Thus their well-being is ultimately tied, by a long string of financial considerations, to the
international corporations that manufacture equipment and chemical compounds. And to
other corporations, which buy their products, barley and spuds and industrially fattened
cattle. Their freedom to act as independent citizens is seriously diminished.

What we commonly call agribusiness runs on a model pushed by those corporations, and
by agricultural schools such as those at the University of California at Davis and Oregon
State University. It's a system ultimately tied together by complexly negotiated strings of
credit and repayment, both psychic and fiscal. Working farmers and ranchers are not
specifically at fault. But there are other ways to organize an agricultural economy. Short-
term efficiency is not the only measure of success.

Lost River suckers (*c'wam*),
Upper Klamath Lake,
Oregon.

8

When I was going to high school in Klamath Falls, a kid off the ranch who wintered in town, friends and I would go out to Klamath Lake in the springtime and snag suckers. We didn't use any bait, just bare treble hooks. Somebody would hang a hook in the side of one of those prehistoric-looking creatures, drag it in, and we'd leave the poor gasping thing with its blowhole mouth on the bank to die. Such were the glories. Who would have thought those suckers would turn up on the endangered species list? Who could imagine their well-being would eventually be of enormous economic consequence in the land of grown-ups?

Who could have imagined, when the first settlers were arriving in their trains of wagons, having smelled the dampness in the air for days before they saw the swamps, that there would be a shortage of water in the Klamath Basin? Or that the Indian tribes, the Klamath and the Hupas, would have an enormous amount to say about its distribution? That they would, by the year 2000, the beginning of the new millennium, be involved in fundamental decisions about the economic future of the Klamath Basin?

Working to rebuild their cultures, the Klamath tribe has used the court system to reestablish their treaty rights as essentially inviolable. Federal courts have ruled that rights to hunt and fish within original reservation boundaries are retained by tribal members. And that their water rights still exist.

Water law in the American West derives from what is called "prior appropriation doctrine." The water rights of whomever first diverted water from a stream for beneficial use take precedence over those of all subsequent users.

Laws grow out of the specific needs and beliefs of a society as it evolves. Water laws in England and the eastern United States followed "riparian doctrine," which acknowledged that water in a stream course is an amenity that enhances the beauty and thus the value of property along the stream.

This was nonsense to miners during the gold rush in California. Water diverted from streams was the essential tool in placer mining technology, thus a commodity. In the mining camp system the first user of in-stream water had an absolute right of continued priority. In times of shortage, users were cut off in their order of priority.

This notion ignored two related principles of riparian water law, the need to conserve water and to maintain in-stream flows. Both are meant to ensure water quality and the continued health of streamside habitats. Nevertheless, in 1855 the Supreme Court of California, in *Irwin v. Phillips,* followed the miners and made "first in time, first in right" the law for California. Before long, prior appropriation was the basis for water law across the arid West.

Federal court support for Native American water rights goes back to 1908 and a confrontation over waters from the Milk River of northern Montana, a clash between a settler named Harry Winters and his neighbors, the Gros Ventre people on the Fort Belknap Reservation. The United States Supreme Court said the Indians had prior claim, and in fact a unique right to the water based on their treaty with the U.S. government.

Reservations had been established as permanent homelands for tribes, with the intent that they become "pastoral and civilized" and give up their nomadic ways. Congress had intended to entitle tribes to water for agricultural, livestock, domestic, recreational, and cultural uses. Courts have understood this to mean the water necessary to irrigate "all practicably irrigable acreage" within the reservation. Courts have also honored many reservation agreements establishing hunting, fishing, gathering, and timber rights. The water needed to satisfy such rights has been quantified as the amount necessary for optimal in-stream flows to sustain fish or riparian areas, not only in terms of quantity but quality.

Tribes are guaranteed water for reasonable future needs. Whether that water had ever been claimed or used by the tribes, or not, is immaterial; the water is there for the Indians whenever they decide to use it. State and local appropriations don't affect native rights, although adjudication of quantities to be delivered to the tribes is a matter to be determined by state courts. (That adjudication process is beginning in the Klamath Basin.)

A landmark decision as to the rights of the Klamath tribe came in 1974, after the termination of their reservation. In *Kimball v. Callahan,* Judge Gus Solomon of the United States District Court for Oregon ruled that people "who were Klamath Indians by ancestry and who elected to withdraw from the tribe pursuant to the Klamath Termination Act and have their interest in tribal property converted to money and paid to them, nevertheless retained treaty rights to hunt, trap, and fish free of state regulations on former Indian land that was sold to pay for their shares in tribal property, including land taken by the United States for national forests and privately owned land on which hunting, trapping, or fishing was permitted." In short, the Termination Act wasn't "a backhanded way of abrogating the hunting and fishing rights of these Indians."

Another landmark decision, involving water rights on a portion of the Williamson River watershed, the *United States of America and the Klamath Indian Tribe v. Ben Adair,* came down in 1984. It determined that the Klamath Indians have a water right with a priority date of time immemorial "to as much water on Reservation lands as they need to protect their hunting and fishing rights." Those rights come before any others.

Glenn and Linda Barrett with
son, Michael, Langell Valley,
Oregon, 1998.

The brute facts are simple: Long ago the federal government awarded the Klamath and the downriver tribes rights to water in the Klamath Basin; those rights still exist. The tribes are determined to exercise them. Other users, economically powerful or not, will have to adjust. The implications for water users in the Klamath Basin are potentially enormous. The Indian rights to unpolluted water to be used in support of endangered fisheries come first. Farms and ranches and wildlife refuges get the rest.

In response to water restrictions during the summer of 1992, Langell Valley irrigators began a lawsuit, which the U.S. Supreme Court decided in their favor, in essence saying that environmentally driven courtroom decisions cannot be made without considering economic impact. The implications of this decision are cloudy, but the irrigators were jubilant. Glenn Barrett, a well-spoken Langell Valley farmer who saw the case through, said, "At least we'll have our say in court."

But like many people in the Klamath Basin, Barrett wants to get the decision-making processes out of the courts. He says, "Klamath people are hungry for education. We're willing to learn. We need to go back to the biologists. Find out the facts, and react with common sense. There's a lot of common ground. We can coexist." In the meantime, in dry years, to ensure that suckers in Lost River and Klamath Lake, and downstream salmon, have enough good water, irrigation ditches may stand empty.

Bare Island,
Upper Klamath Lake,
Oregon.

Elwood Miller, in the Klamath tribal offices at Chiloquin, said science has validated traditional tribal knowledge. Everything in a watershed connects. The Klamath is endangered from the top of the system to the bottom, from bull trout in Sycan to vanishing salmon in the lower river.

The tribes, with their preeminent water rights, Miller said, want to deal as generously as possible with the interests of agriculture. "We don't want to be adversaries. We want to find a balance. We don't want to hurt anybody. But our tribal economy crashed a long time ago. We want to bring it back. And water is our livelihood. We want our fish back. The suckers and the salmon. I've heard that since I was a boy listening to the old men. We don't want to take water away from people. We'd like to find solutions for everybody's problems. But we'll wrap our arms around what's necessary."

The Reclamation Service in the early days of the Klamath Project promised farmers water they had no assurance of receiving, and the agency called no attention to the fact of rights guaranteed to the tribes. That oversight, stupid or duplicitous, whatever, will beyond doubt influence solutions to water problems in the Klamath Basin. But it is not the fault of people from the Klamath tribes.

Anger should be directed toward the old-time Reclamation Service, who got the farmers into this situation, who built the basis for the enormous enterprise that is agribusiness in the Klamath Basin on the use of water that was not theirs to give away. Maybe, we think, those old-line bureaucrats imagined the tribes were moribund and would vanish. No doubt some bureaucrats were busy building kingdoms. The injustices historically connected to the Bureau of Reclamation's administration of Native American waters have been widely recognized, for instance by the National Water Commission, reporting to the president and Congress in 1973:

> The United States was pursuing a policy of encouraging the settlement of the West and the creation of family-sized farms on its arid lands. In retrospect, it can be seen that this policy was pursued with little or no regard for Indian water rights and the *Winters* doctrine. With the encouragement, or at least the cooperation, of the Secretary of Interior—the very office entrusted with the protection of all Indian rights—many large irrigation projects were constructed on streams that flowed through or bordered on Indian Reservations, sometimes above and often below the Reservations. With few exceptions, the projects were planned and built by the Federal Government without any attempt to define, let alone protect, prior rights that Indian tribes might have had to the waters used for the projects. In the history of the United States Government's treatment of Indian tribes, its failure to protect Indian water rights on the Reservations it set aside for them is one of the sorrier chapters.

Jeff Mitchell, Klamath tribal chairman, in an open letter to the Klamath Basin community published in the Klamath Falls *Herald and News* in September 1997, said,

Jeff Mitchell, chairman of the
Klamath tribes, overlooking
Upper Klamath Lake at Modoc
Point Rim, Klamath Basin,
Oregon, 1998.

The water adjudication process is a zero sum game with only a narrow focus on "winner" and "losers." Without a broader mandate to deal with water shortages, resource depletion, and habitat restoration, the adjudication process will not address the continuing threat to our Basin's economy, community and natural resources brought about by inadequate water supply.

Resolution of water rights alone will never lead to real solutions that meet all parties [*sic*] water resource interests.

Mitchell advocates strong local involvement in the adjudication processes:

Negotiations, framed and controlled by the Basin's water interests, will allow for far greater regional control and a solution sensitive to all interests' concerns.

Negotiations have the potential to break down walls of distrust, and build better relationships among the participants because of their cooperative structure. And they are designed to be open to all the interests in our community.

Ultimately, the Klamath Tribes believe the water settlement negotiation process is the best available forum for resolving Basin water issues.

This sounds supremely reasonable, but many citizens in the Klamath Basin are not accustomed to listening when the tribes speak. They want to blame their troubles on the Indians. People say the tribes are using their leverage to build a power base, which is likely true. Why not? That's clearly been the white agenda for a hundred years.

"They shoot pregnant does out of season," a white rancher told me. "Traditional people never did that."

"They don't give a damn about conservation. They catch enough trout to fill a barley sack."

It's said white lawyers are manipulating the tribes. To what point? This small-minded grousing, attacking people whom many in the basin want to understand as powerless, is useless in any long run. The tribes claim to believe in renewal and say they are willing to negotiate. And negotiations are under way. It's a start, seemingly based on an impulse to heal. School-yard posturing by whites is endlessly counterproductive, a way of avoiding responsibility.

As quantification of water rights, in state courts, comes up for adjudication, lawyers are preparing for war. Let's hope that, as Jeff Mitchell suggested, the battles can be settled in negotiation, citizen to citizen. The adjudication processes might kick the processes of communality into gear. Before the aggrieved parties set themselves up for more legal fees, they ought to try talking across a table, and see if they can't work out something that could be followed by a handshake. But, at present, lawyers—some of them very adept and Native American—are running the show.

A white trapper poses with pelts of coyote, bobcat, and skunk. Photograph by Maud Baldwin. Courtesy of The Klamath County Museum.

Bogus Creek,
Klamath River,
California

9

GRIDLOCK

The earth-filled Fort Peck Dam, built by the Bureau of Reclamation in the 1930s to back up a 140-mile reservoir in Montana, is the largest structure anywhere on earth, except for the Great Wall of China, which took a thousand years to build.

In 1936 the Bureau of Reclamation was simultaneously constructing the four largest concrete dams ever built—Hoover on the Colorado, Shasta on the Sacramento, and Bonneville and Grand Coulee on the Columbia. Over forty years, thirteen enormous dams were built on the Columbia. And twenty-three more dams, many of them huge, were built on tributaries like the Deschutes and the Clearwater and the Santiam and the Willamette.

The Bureau of Reclamation is the greatest builder in the history of humankind. But its success story ran aground in the 1960s, when it became obvious that there wasn't enough water in the Colorado River to meet the needs of both Southern California and Arizona.

Reclamation built the Glen Canyon Dam on the Colorado amid considerable controversy, and followed that by proposing two more dams, in the Grand Canyon. Public opposition, orchestrated by David Brower of the Sierra Club, was enormous. Engineering, the national public said, wasn't the answer to every problem. Particularly engineering that proposed to sacrifice a national treasure like the Grand Canyon. In a public debate about which was more valuable, irrigation water for Southern California and Arizona, or the Grand Canyon, the canyon won, going away. The Bureau had finally overplayed its hand. Their engineers, used to having their way with western watershed developments, were taken by surprise.

In that same era another Bureau scheme to provide irrigation water for Southern California involved damming the Klamath River twelve miles up from the Pacific, since the river was said to be "wasting" an estimated 12,000,000 acre-feet of water into the sea. The great dam, to be called Ah Pah, would stand 813 feet high and back water seventy miles up the Klamath and forty miles up the Trinity to form a reservoir with 15,050,000 acre-feet of storage capacity. The proposed Trinity Tunnel, a horseshoe seventy miles long and thirty-seven feet in diameter, would carry water to the Sacramento Valley. Canals, aqueducts, and other tunnels, including the proposed forty-mile Tehachapi Tunnel, would carry the water to the Los Angeles basin. All at a cost of something like $3.5 billion. This, of course, without a seeming thought to the fact that the homeland of the people who owned much of the water, the Hupa Indians, was going to be forever flooded. It's not hard to understand why Indians along the Klamath River are suspicious of various white governmental water-management schemes.

The Klamath River project probably could have been brought off. The Klamath wasn't the Grand Canyon, the Hupa were an obscure, powerless people who might have been easily manipulated, and Congress was used to giving Reclamation funds to build whatever it wanted, no matter the price.

But leaders at the Bureau weren't used to being challenged. They weren't used to defending the value of ever-larger watershed development; they thought their hegemony would go on forever; they thought they could get to the Klamath when they wanted. The Bureau didn't understand that its moment had passed; its momentum was gone; overweening behavior no longer suited the national mood.

By the late 1960s American values were swiftly changing. The nation had endured the agonies of the civil rights movement and the Kennedy and Martin Luther King assassinations, and was weathering the defeat to our national sense of purpose that was the Vietnam War. The nation was beginning to turn its mind toward taking care, preserving what it had. As the national situation changed, sentiment about western land use policies began changing. The settlement of the West, the years of national expansion, conquering native peoples, railroad and dam building, vast mining and timbering, irrigation projects, these were ending. The conquest of nature in American arid lands was over. The settlers had come, the plow grounds were plowed. A new era was beginning.

Both Teddy Roosevelt and Franklin Delano Roosevelt wanted to be remembered as conservationists and developers. The inherently conflicted agendas they advocated are reflected in the bureaucracies attempting to deal with watershed problems in the Klamath Basin. The consequences are an endless sea of paperwork and chains of administrative hierarchy in service of objectives that are at best imprecisely defined. No wonder state and federal bureaucracies in the American West are so widely understood as dysfunctional. Ranchers and farmers trying to initiate restorative projects find they are caught in a webwork of rules invented by people who don't live inside the territory and often don't have much sense of local rhythms or ecologies. As a result there is in local communities, and among many thinkers across the American West, a sentiment that the agencies ought to be simply shut down: "Get the government out of our hair." Return control of land, water, and other resources to local citizens. Democratize the processes. Give back our freedoms.

Absolute local and regional self-determination is a concept articulated in the furious, semi-incoherent rantings of antitax "Freemen" and in the careful reasoning of libertarians in towns across the West. My Missoula ex-mayor and friend, Dan Kemmis, recently wrote that "the West's best observers, from Jefferson to Frederick Jackson Turner, from John Wesley Powell to Wallace Stegner have always detected some emanation of democratic spirit from the western landscape. A key component . . . is a refusal to be trapped in box canyons of

"We end, I think, at what might be called the standard paradox of the twentieth century: our tools are better than we are, and grow better faster than we do. They suffice to crack the atom, to command the tides. But they do not suffice for the oldest task in human history: to live on a piece of land without spoiling it."

any kind." Which is sort of true. But we also have to have legal mechanisms to control agribusiness, timber-cutting outfits, and mining corporations, which have a history of throwing their economic weight around, hoodwinking citizens, and buying politicians in order to have their imperial way. Without control by public agencies, international corporations would likely take over a variety of Klamath Basin public land enterprises. "All the lease lands in the Tule Lake Basin," a man told me. "Birds and everything."

Lands owned by the public and managed by the Forest Service, the Bureau of Land Management, the Bureau of National Parks and Monuments, and the U.S. Fish and Wildlife Service are common national property, an enormous publicly owned commons. American citizens in Utah and Louisiana and Vermont think the flights of migrating waterbirds in the Klamath Basin are their responsibility. The Klamath Basin is a national treasure, like the Hudson River, the Mississippi, or the Everglades. Much of it belongs to citizens everywhere. Regulatory agencies represent the interests of that citizenry. They are hired to protect my interests in the Everglades, although I've never lived in Florida, and the interests of everyone else. They are also hired to protect my interests in the Klamath watershed even though I live in Montana.

The agencies are asked to do their jobs inside a system approaching gridlock. A simple list of conflicting and competing country and state and federal jurisdictional and administrative entities operating in the Klamath Basin is enough to drive the most hardened bureaucrat (not to speak of ranchers and farmers) into catatonia. There's the U.S. Fish and Wildlife Service, with offices in the Tule Lake Basin and Portland; the Bureau of Reclamation, with offices in Klamath Falls, Sacramento, and (in regard to water being delivered over the Cascade ridge into the Rogue River system) Boise; the Forest Service, with Winema National Forest offices in Klamath Falls and regional Forest Service offices in Sacramento and Portland; the Bureau of Indian Affairs offices in Portland (the Klamath tribes) and Sacramento (California tribes); the Bureau of Land Management, headquartered in Portland; the Environmental Protection Agency for Oregon, headquartered in Seattle; the National Marine Fisheries in Long Beach; and even the National Park Service (Crater Lake). And groups like the Nature Conservancy and Trout Unlimited and the National Audubon Society and the Sierra Club and the Oregon Natural Resource Council, all of whom also generate their own agendas and paperwork. Bud Ullman, an attorney for the Klamath tribes, summed it up when he told me that these jurisdictions and power bases are "arbitrary but nonetheless real. A fact of life."

Interwoven areas of authority stand in the way of bureaucratic efficiency and bring farmers and ranchers, trying to get the crops in and the cows fed, trying to survive inside a thicket of rules and paperwork, to throw up their hands. Good ideas, good for the land, good for the community, are abandoned. The only helping hands out there for hire, as people try to work within the maze, belong to lawyers. It's not that people in the agencies don't understand that this system is often close to impenetrable and don't want to see it simplified. Forest Service officials repeatedly ask Congress to streamline procedures. But there's not much they can do until legislation reforming their structures is enacted.

Congress doesn't seem inclined to act, because of pressure from timber industry corporations who've had western senators (and thus the Forest Service) in their pockets for a long time and don't want the boat rocked. This is true despite endless complaining about the old-growth timber they haven't got to log yet. The self-interested and wealthy get lawyers, and those simply trying to do some good work most often don't. The result is both antiprogressive and antidemocratic. Since there is no realistic chance that society will shut down these bureaucracies, or even simplify the system, what we need is help for on-the-ground people, with the paperwork if nothing more.

The Forest Service, the U.S. Fish and Wildlife Service, and their bureaucracies are absolutely necessary. But a lot of people think they could make a stronger show of doing their jobs. It would help in the Klamath Basin if the Bureau of Reclamation would articulate its ideologies and consequent set of objectives in public, in precise language. But in a system in which agencies are pressured by a variety of local, national, and international economic-power brokers while their bosses—Congress, the president, and ultimately the court system—are constantly revising their opinions, that's close to impossible.

The agencies would no doubt find their jobs a lot easier if both the local and national citizenry made a better show of deciding what it is we want. We send them contradictory messages. We love the sight of waterbirds in migration but we want to farm with toxic chemicals in the vicinity of our wildlife refuges; we want to preserve farmlands but we demand the right to subdivide our own property; we love remnant stands of old-growth yellow pine but we want to build wooden houses. We want to have our cake and eat it. We eat ourselves alive.

HOME RULE

Laurence Shaw, founder of the Modoc Lumber Company, died at the age of eighty-nine in late February 1998. Modoc was one of the top one hundred lumber producers in the country, and one of the top one hundred privately held companies in Oregon. In the 1950s, when the Klamath Indian Reservation was terminated, Shaw organized local business leaders to advocate creation of Winema National Forest and ensured that reservation forestlands would not be sold to out-of-Oregon corporations. Thus, he did good work on behalf of the Klamath Basin timber industry, and on behalf of his own business. And his efforts resulted in a lot of jobs in Klamath Falls. Shaw was also a very active philanthropist, with a

strong interest in local history. The Shaw Library at the Oregon Technical Institute in Klamath Falls is a prime repository for regional archives. Shaw can be thought to have had an exemplary private and public career. But his was also a ruling-class career. Problem-solving leadership in the Klamath Basin has traditionally been generated inside a small group of the economically privileged.

Throughout history, as John Wesley Powell pointed out, public works have often been successful as a result of profoundly antidemocratic processes. Private fortunes, in the West, have been amassed by manipulation of publicly funded processes like Forest Service timber sales and by the use of irrigated lands created by Bureau of Reclamation projects. The means

The early days of logging were a time of large trees and hand tools. Photograph by Darius Kinsey. Courtesy of The Klamath County Museum.

"A system of conservation based solely on economic self-interest is hopelessly lopsided. It tends to ignore, and thus eventually to eliminate, many elements in the land community that lack commercial value, but that are essential to its healthy functioning."

of production often, if not inevitably, accumulate in the hands of operators who are persistent and work hard to get what they want. But that doesn't mean those operators are interested in negotiating the whimsies of a truly democratic venue. They like to lock up a sure thing. Who could blame them?

That the Klamath Basin is home to a democratic society of property-owning ranchers and farmers is also clear. Go have a meal in a cafe in Merrill or Fort Klamath and you will see them talking and settling local problems. But working-class citizens aren't often invited to ultimate decision-making parties, although they also have an obvious stake in the local economy.

The existence of a decision-making class is a fact most Americans don't like to acknowledge. In a rigorously democratic society, political power is not supposed to gather in the hands of individuals and institutions who've never been subjected to electoral processes.

For decades, timber cutting and milling were the prime economic activities in the Klamath Basin. Logging corporations and companies called a lot of economic and political shots. Now the Modoc Lumber Company mill on Lake Ewauna, and the Weyerhauser mill, reputed to have been the world's largest pine mill, are gone. Logging and timber milling are no longer the economic centerpieces in the Klamath Basin.

Large agriculturalists, and representatives of the banks and seed and chemical and machinery companies that supply their needs, constitute another self-serving consortium. But as their ways of doing business are challenged, their hegemony is passing. This doesn't necessarily cause a lot of sadness around Klamath Falls. Classic resentments abound. "Those big-shot farmers," a man told me, "are due to eat some crow."

As another ruling class passes on, the economy becomes more diversified. This means, at least in theory, that it will be more resilient, and stable. Cow prices and fluctuations in the potato and barley markets won't matter so much to downtown merchants. The job market will be steadier.

Among the major players in the Klamath economy these days are Aqua Glass, a manufacturer of shower stalls, tubs, and basins; and Sykes, a computer programming company whose prime customer is Disney; and a trio of specialty forest products manufacturers, Columbia Plywood, Collins Forest Products, and Jeld-Win, Incorporated.

Jeld-Win, which manufactures doors and windows, was in 1998 the largest privately held company in Oregon. It's exactly the sort of "value added" enterprise the West needs (in-

stead of unmilled timber being shipped to Japan, manufacturing is done locally; thus value is added and the hometown economy is given a serious boost). But Jeld-Win also has other irons in the fire. They are developing land on the west side of Klamath Lake into a high-end, golf-centered community called the Running Y Ranch Resort—a first-rate Arnold Palmer course, condos, nine hundred homes, amenities. I've played the golf course—it's a dandy.

The whole package will bring a lot of money into the Klamath Basin. Another recreational project, a destination ski resort that will be built on nearby Pelican Butte, if environmentalist objections, based mainly on water quality and wildlife habitat issues, are solved (Jeld-Win is working on it), will bring more. The Running Y and Pelican Butte could generate a kind of synergistic energy, each feeding on the other. It's happened in a lot of places around the West, recently in Bend. People in Klamath Falls would like to share the prosperity. But I couldn't get anybody to talk about what might become of the aspen-framed parkland grazing country north of Klamath Lake. It's easy to imagine serious golf courses up there, fertilizers and pesticides on the fairways and greens, a run of condos, and fished-out streams.

Floating the logs downstream was the best way to reach a sawmill in the days before the railroad. Photograph by Maud Baldwin. Courtesy of The Klamath County Museum.

According to Forest Service estimates, recreation in national forests will be bringing in $110.7 billion of revenue annually by the year 2000, opposed to $3.5 billion from timber contracts. Money talks, and it's talking hiking, golfing, and skiing, not logging or ranching or farming. Solutions to regional economic troubles designed to generate a fountain of tourist money in the Klamath Basin, along with a lot of service (servant) jobs.

Longtime citizens in Bend, Moab, Jackson Hole, Park City, and Aspen feel their communities have at least partway dissolved in the acid of tourist-servicing commercialism. Many feel they are worse off.

Service jobs don't pay like timber falling. On the other hand, a service economy generates many such jobs and can be very important to overall community prosperity. But economic and emotional distances between haves and have-nots are usually exacerbated in communities that have made the transition to a largely service economy. This is bad for all concerned, since the source of enduring prosperity is citizen willingness to take part in the processes of communality, like smiling at one another and keeping the streets clean.

Communities that feel good about themselves tend to be understood as good places to live and do business. New businesses and voters, thus money, flow uphill to them. Those that thrive over time try to ensure the well-being of citizens by providing first-rate schools and parks, public health facilities, and strong welfare programs. Impoverished citizens are given ladders up out of their neediness, thus making sure the community has a constant source of renewed vitality.

Another central enterprise driving the economic structure in the Klamath Basin is Cell Tech, Incorporated, which harvests algae from Klamath Lake and processes it into organic health-food supplements. In 1996, doing business out of existing buildings, employing about 450 locals, selling products exclusively through a network of share-holding distributors, Cell Tech generated some $200 million, equaling the gross income from farming in Tule Lake and Lower Klamath Basins.

But algae from Agency Lake was found to contain microcystin, a liver toxin. In October 1997, the Oregon Department of Agriculture established a limit of one part per million of microcystin in blue-green algae products. It's questionable if parts per million can even be measured with existing technologies. But there's no doubt it was a public-relations disaster for Cell Tech. Jim Carpenter, company spokesman, said, "It's devastating. We lost $100 million in gross income over this." Carpenter is a very quick study who, inside the traditional economic atmosphere of the Klamath Basin, wears the mantle of semi-hippy success lightly. He takes care of business, for Cell Tech and the community, and sells a lot of product along the way.

Cell Tech is studying markets for products like algae-based organic fertilizers and livestock feed additives. Farming in the future (or so people like me want to believe) is likely to be increasingly centered on the use of organics to stimulate production and control weeds and pests. Agricultural product corporations and chemical companies will eventually recognize the necessity of throwing the power of their funding into organic research (or, more probably, public awareness will force them to it). When that time comes, an international market for algae-based organic soil additives and fertilizers will likely generate a lot of cash. The Klamath Basin might explode with prosperity—local wealth and good jobs generated by environmentally responsible agriculture.

The political power of the economically privileged in the United States, the American West, and the Klamath Basin is a fact of life. Such traditional leadership is not necessarily a bad thing if acknowledged, if the agendas they put forward are talked about in specific detail and openly, on the streets and in cafes, in all varieties of public forums and in the various media, newspapers and television, a lot.

And, such traditional leadership is not a bad thing if the privileged participate in these discussions and are responsive to what they get as feedback from the local community, if the processes are ultimately democratic, and subject to the public will.

The possibility of developing a tourist-centered economy in Klamath Falls ought to be given intensive public scrutiny, rather than simply publicized and pushed by those who stand to profit most. Old solutions—money and jobs, reinvented by business leaders—still work. But trickle-down economics don't often serve the poor, like the floating population of visible but politically silent laboring people from Latin America and Asia, who do much of the farmwork in the Klamath Basin. And most citizens want a voice in determining public agendas.

Michael Croy, wild
mushroom scout and broker,
Dorris, California, 1997.

Bill Turnock, former owner
of the Sycan Springs Trout
Farm, Beatty, Oregon, 1998.

Michelle and Jennifer Elder
and their Chihuahua, Peanut,
Dorris, California, 1998.

Marvin Krebs, Donna and
Harley Krebs, Modoc
National Forest, California,
1998. The Krebses, in their
lifetime, have chopped,
split, and hauled over
26,000 cords of wood.

Eddie Richardson *(right)* and
his assistant, Larry Miller Jr.,
Poe Valley, Oregon, 1998.

Mary Jane and Rudolph
Paygr, retired farmers, Malin,
Oregon, 1998. Rudy Paygr
was the first child born to the
Czech community in Malin.

Larry Vercellotti, Indian
Tom Lake, California, 1998.
Black Limousin bulls are part
of Vercellotti's cow-calf
operation.

Barry Brennan, log dump
supervisor at Columbia
Plywood, rides the log bronc
Klamath, Klamath River,
Oregon, 1998. Log rafts are
moved by these little vessels.

Laurie and Jerry Noakes,
Macdoel, California, 1998.
Jerry ranches, hauls cattle, and
moves earth for wetland
restoration projects.

Pat Collins, Lower Klamath
Lake, California, 1998.
Collins traps nonnative
muskrats along dikes and
ditches for the U.S. Fish
and Wildlife Service.

Pedro Garcias, Indian Tom
Lake, California, 1998.
Before the collapse of the
Mexican economy in the
nineties, Garcias owned and
operated a large dairy in
Guadalajara.

Cathy Hanscom at home,
near Upper Klamath Lake,
Oregon, 1998. Hanscom
dries and markets flowers
grown in her two-acre
garden.

Ross' geese,
Lower Klamath Lake,
California.

10

CHEMICALS

In the 1930s, a little more than a hundred miles to the east of the Klamath Basin, in Warner Valley, my father was at work on a private reclamation project, building miles of dikes, irrigation canals, and pumping plants, working eighteen hours a day to break out new peat plow-grounds. Managing the system he built was work I inherited and loved for a long time. But in 1962, still a young man trying to prove himself, I was profoundly spooked by my reading of *Silent Spring,* by Rachel Carson. So were many others. In 1992 it was voted the most influential American book published in the last fifty years. The reasons for my spookiness were simple. Carson, writing primarily about the toxic results of chemicals commonly used in large-scale farming, might have been talking about the ways my family used chemical fertilizers and pesticides in our farming operations.

Carson described a die-off of fish-eating birds in Tule Lake and Lower Klamath Lake that could only be attributed to the buildup of toxic chemicals through accumulation in runoff water from treated farmlands: "Such poisoning of waters set aside for conservation purposes could have consequences felt by . . . everyone to whom the sight and sound of drifting ribbons of waterfowl across an evening sky are precious." She spoke of a "chain of poisoning" in various western waters, a "house-that-Jack-built sequence," in which carnivores eat smaller carnivores that eat herbivores that eat plankton that "absorbed the poison from the water."

Deploring "the deliberate introduction of poisons" into the environment in an "era dominated by industry," she said the public was "fed little tranquilizing pills of half-truth." Writing about the industrialization of agriculture, attempts to control complex in-the-ground chemical processes, she connected such overweening behavior to unintended results like the poisoning of the waterbirds. Carson spoke of "fanatic zeal" on the part of single-crop agriculturalists and asked if such practices were "wise or desirable," and reminded us that "in nature nothing exists alone." She summed up by saying, "The control of nature is a phrase conceived in arrogance, born in the Neanderthal age of biology and philosophy, when it was supposed that nature exists for the convenience of man."

Rereading *Silent Spring,* I'm reminded of the young farmer I was, in the emotionally and intellectually isolated faraway land that was Warner Valley in the years before computers and 150 channels of television, and of the sense of betrayal and humiliation I felt while absorbing what she had to say, the interrelated chemical and moral realities she laid out so clearly in that matter-of-fact tone.

Farming was my life, and I loved it. Farming was a version of God's work, making the earth orderly, inciting it to produce food. I hated what Rachel Carson was saying—that in following exactly the practices I'd been taught in ag school at Oregon State University, I was actively participating in the poisoning of everything I held sacred—the peat soils, the green-winged teal and Canadian honkers, my children. Coming to terms with that news led me to eventually, over decades, recognize the complexity of my allegiances. Caring for crops as they grow toward the reward of harvest, within specific particularities of soil and weather, is I think for most farmers much the same as making art. Good farming, I'm willing to say without irony, is a form of artistry.

But I also loved the disorderly magnificence of white snow geese by the clamoring thousands rising from barley stubble to an overcast November afternoon. Contrary loves, according to the message in *Silent Spring*. Sounds like a country and western song, and it sort of worked out that way in my life. Escaping that classical double bind, before another half dozen years got away, I fled. I went off to be reeducated, and to make my life at universities. I learned to live in what's best thought of as a network of the like-minded rather than a specifically located community. The implications turn out to be quite political. My allegiances tend to be generated by ideas centered on taking care of our ultimate commons, life on earth. People like me are everywhere. We're both idealists and elitists. We tend to be true believers and to advocate rethinking societal values. We are unwilling to rely on the future to solve the problems our society is making for itself. We want solutions now. Business as usual, we think, won't do. There are more and more of us all the time.

Conservation activists are often willing to interfere in local day-to-day economic transactions while acting on behalf of habitats and creatures. Humans, they say, are empowered to take care of themselves. Citizens who are primarily interested in the success of their communities are infuriated. They feel invaded by people who don't care a damn about their economic well-being. Often, they're right, at least in the short term.

In 1993 a man named Wendell Wood moved into a house on Lakeshore Drive along Klamath Lake just north of Klamath Falls. Wood represents the Oregon Natural Resource Council (ONRC), a group self-described as an "Aggressive Defender of Oregon's Wild Lands." Through his work and his willingness to sue any environmental offender, Wood has become the most reviled and resented man in the Klamath Basin. He doesn't seem to care. His indifference to local politics makes him enormously powerful. The source of his power, his environmentalist constituency, mostly lives outside the basin.

Wendell Wood and I met for an hour or so in the late afternoon of a pretty autumn day

in Moore Park, on the north side of Klamath Falls near the place where the water of the lake falls away into the Link River. My grandparents used to take me there when I was a child to visit a primitive zoo. I think I recall a skinny bear in a cage. Wendell Wood and I sat at a picnic table near a fountain built of archeological artifacts, stone bowls and pestles found in the basin. The lawns were mowed, fall flowers were in bloom, but the tennis courts were empty. The afternoon seemed satisfied with itself.

A small, intense man, Wendell Wood looked to be a bookish fellow in the mostly good-old-boys culture of the Klamath Basin. He is a professional environmentalist. Hard-line. He asked what kind of story I was intending to tell. About citizens seeking agreement, I said, about ways of solving intertwined ecological and social problems. It looked to me, I said, like the trouble in the Klamath Basin could be worked through without any big losers.

Tundra swan, Tule Lake, California.

"You've been talking to the compromisers," Wendell Wood said. The action I'd guess Wendell Wood finds most deplorable is compromise in regard to preserving natural processes. The primary weapon Wood uses in his efforts to protect the environment is the Endangered Species Act. In 1993 Wood got hold of records indicating that the U.S. Fish and Wildlife Service and the Bureau of Reclamation had not been enforcing federal pesticide rules on the leased farmlands within the refuges for more than thirty years. The U.S. Fish and Wildlife Service, decades after *Silent Spring,* seemed to still be allowing farmers to contaminate the water in wildlife refuges with toxic pesticides.

The agencies were operating within rules they had established in response to the Kuchel Act of 1964. But if they weren't enforcing federal pesticide guidelines—having yielded to pressure from agricultural interests, satisfying the people they had to deal with on a day-to-day basis—the agencies were clearly failing to do their job in a responsible manner. And waterfowl numbers, particularly in the Tule Lake National Wildlife Refuge, were falling. Seriously. Pesticide contamination was certainly a possible reason why.

In February 1994, the Northwest Coalition for Alternatives to Pesticides and the ONRC filed notice of intent to sue over federal failure to enforce pesticide regulations. In an out-of-court settlement, the Bureau of Reclamation agreed to require farmers to get permission to use federally restricted pesticides. The Bureau would also consult with biologists on possible ways those chemicals might affect threatened and endangered species. But the fallout was just beginning.

On October 9, 1997, President Clinton signed the National Wildlife System Improvement Act of 1997, which spells out the System's mission, requires public review of decisions about what activities will be allowed on refuges, and specifies that, while wildlife conservation is the highest priority of the refuges, wildlife-related recreation must take priority over nonwildlife uses of the refuges. The act says that "the mission of the system is to administer a national network of lands and waters for the conservation, management, and where appropriate, restoration of the fish, wildlife, and plant resources and their habitats within the United States for the benefit of present and future generations of Americans."

While recognizing that the Tule Lake and Lower Klamath refuges are administered under the Kuchel Act ("for the major purpose of waterfowl management, but with full consideration to optimal agricultural use"), the language of the act emphasizes "recreation" and "restoration." The bill requires the U.S. Fish and Wildlife Service to make in writing compatibility determinations on whether or not specific activities can be allowed on refuges, allow public review of the decisions, periodically review these decisions, and prepare "comprehensive conservation plans" for each refuge with full public involvement.

In July 1998, in response to the 1997 Act and to requirements in the Endangered Species Act that the agency not jeopardize the existence of endangered or threatened species or their habitats, the U.S. Fish and Wildlife Service issued a draft *Environmental Assessment of an Integrated Pest Management Plan for the Klamath Refuges.*

The plan says it's the policy of the U.S. Fish and Wildlife Service to "eliminate unnecessary use of pesticides by implementing integrated pest management techniques and by selecting crops that are beneficial to fish and wildlife but do not require pesticides." It also quotes the agency's administrative manual on pest management policy and responsibilities,

saying, "Management practices, including farming programs, will be examined to ensure that 1) they have a high value for fish and wildlife resources, 2) they do not encourage the exposure of pathogens or development of disease vectors that affect fish or wildlife resources, and that 3) they require minimal or no application of hazardous chemicals." The pesticide use manual produced by the Department of Interior says, "Pesticides may be used in habitats involving endangered or threatened animal or plant species only after it is determined that such use will not adversely affect the species or its critical habitat." These mission statements, in the working out, seem to have historically been wide open to local interpretation. Who, for instance, gets to decide that a specific pesticide use "will not adversely affect the species or its critical habitat"? If we believe what scientists since Aldo Leopold have told us about the interwoven nature of life, any pesticide use will affect local habitat. Pesticide-use decisions, common sense indicates, should not turn on evidence of pesticide pollution as judged by effects on local creatures, but on whether there is any *possibility* of pollution. Any risk is too much.

Great egret,
Sycan Marsh,
Oregon.

Bald eagles,
Tule Lake, California.

Bald eagles and peregrine falcons that visit the basin, and Lost River and shortnose suckers, the two species of suckers in the Lost River drainage (including the Tule Lake sumps), have been listed as threatened or endangered. This would seem clear reason to completely eliminate the use of pesticides on the lease lands. But because of local economic pressures, pesticide use has been continually allowed on the Klamath refuges. That's the basis for a building public relations disaster for the U.S. Fish and Wildlife Service and the Bureau of Reclamation.

In January 1998, scoping meetings were held to define lease-land pesticide-use issues. Farmers, conservationists, and personnel from the two agencies came up with a list of twenty-three. Agency personnel condensed this list to a fundamental three.

1. Income to individuals, the county, and the local economy might be lost by implementing the integrated pest management plan.
2. Without integrated pest management (IPM), the risk to endangered or threatened species (the two species of suckers, peregrine falcons, bald eagles) and other wildlife might be increased by the use of pesticides as the primary form of pest control.
3. Without IPM, soil, water, and air quality may be degraded both on and off the refuge by continued use of pesticides on the refuge.

In response to these issues, the agencies proposed four alternative courses of action.

1. No action: a continuation of current management by agencies and current practices by growers.
2. Phased integrated pest management program (preferred alternative): use of pesticides as a last line of defense against pests, not the first line of control. It involves a combination of cultivation (and other cultural) practices, and biological and chemical pest controls to reduce reliance on pesticides.
3. Modified IPM program: the same as alternative 2, except that all IPM techniques would have to be proven effective in the Klamath Basin prior to use on the wildlife refuges.
4. Transition from synthetic pesticide use to long-term organic growing methods.

Pesticide use would be prohibited except in emergencies, as when fish, wildlife, or their habitats were threatened by a pest. Or in public health emergencies. Grower practices would be examined to ensure their benefit to wildlife. Harvest times would be keyed to waterfowl nesting, cover, and forage needs. As pest-resistant varieties of crops were developed and new technologies and biochemicals became available, aspects of each would be incorporated into growing operations. In the long run it is assumed that most lease-land growers would convert to organic practices to profit from this "more exclusive marketing niche."

Several more radical alternatives were considered but dismissed, including no regulation of pesticides, removal of lease lands from the national wildlife refuges, restoration of all

Sandhill crane colt, Lower Klamath Lake, California.

wetlands and elimination of lease-land farming, and short-term transition from the existing lease-land program to organic farming. Each is in violation of national policies or—in the language of the integrated pest management plan—is "presently seen as impractical due to local economic considerations."

The list of pesticides permitted for use on the wildlife refuge lease lands in 1998, as reported in the *Oregonian* in July 1998, includes

> Lorsban: An organophosphate pesticide that acts as a nerve toxin. Used to control maggots in crops. Extremely toxic to fish, including the endangered suckers that frequent the Tule Lake National Wildlife Refuge.
>
> Disyston: A pesticide used to control aphids on barley grown on refuge land. The pesticide is toxic to birds, which must be hazed from fields prior to pesticide application. The pesticide can also accumulate in insects such as grasshoppers, which are a food source for birds. These insects can then prove toxic to birds.
>
> Ponce: A pesticide used to control cutworms in potatoes. If it drifts into the water, it can be toxic to fish. Refuge officials require wide buffers between sprayed fields and fish-bearing waterways.

Allen Ardoin, who served on Interior Department teams responsible for approving pesticide use on the federal refuges, was quoted in the *Oregonian* in July 1998 as saying, "You don't use toxic chemicals on a bird refuge. By God, I stand on that one. It's about as simple as you can get."

On a drive through the Tule Lake lease lands, across the deep peat soils of what was once lake bottom, I asked Jim Hainline, whose opinions I had learned to trust, how use of pesticides could be justified in a wildlife refuge. Hainline told me there was little evidence of chemical contamination in the Tule Lake sumps, and that almost no wildlife mortality in the Tule Lake and Klamath refuges could be traced to chemicals. Pesticides are very expensive. For that reason if no other, they are applied in dosages that are immediately absorbed by crops. Monitoring pesticide application, Hainline said, was extraordinarily rigorous. Almost none gets into the water. But, of course, any at all is way too much.

Jim Hainline was quoted in a July 1, 1998, Associated Press story about the Wilderness Society listing of the Klamath refuges as being among the fifteen most threatened federal wildlands in the United States. In the story he "disputed the society's 'bleak' picture of the area and said that while DDT was once a problem, other pesticides have not proven harmful to wildlife. 'We don't deny the fact that the stuff is out there and people are using it, but we haven't found evidence that it is creating problems for us. . . . The only mortalities we've had,' Hainline said, 'have been the result of accidents or bad judgement.'" But chemical-use mortalities of any kind seem inexcusable on a wildlife refuge.

Evidence of pesticides in watersheds ought to be unthinkable, and not only on wildlife refuges. I mean anywhere. Do any of us want such stuff in our water?

On the other hand, it's probably impossible at present, given the intractable nature of late blight in potatoes (the cause of the "potato famine" in Ireland 150 years ago), to raise potatoes without fungicides. And potatoes produce twice as much food per acre as wheat or rice. Farmers say they are trying to feed everybody. But, given present-day food surpluses, it's not an argument that carries much weight (we don't need more food, we need a more efficient distribution system).

Soils like those farmed in Klamath Basin, without counting roots, contain more living biomass below the surface than above. A square meter of dry grassland peat soil contains billions of bacteria, millions of fungi, thousands of spiders and ants and beetles and their larvae, earthworms, slugs, snails, and millions of nematodes. And lots more, all constantly interacting with one another, trading organic compounds, generating and using energies. Good soils are made up of a lot more than dirt. Soils in which these creatures have stopped doing business, in which these processes have ceased, is called lifeless.

Responsible agriculture involves caring for the organisms that both create and are our soils. But we're spending this inheritance at a phenomenal rate. Erosion exceeds soil formation by a factor of thirty. For every bushel of Iowa corn we spend two bushels of soil (after one century of farming, American tallgrass prairie soils, as rich as any, are half gone). Using petroleum and chemicals we give seedlings in our dying soils a jolt, but we don't return any of the trace elements needed for plant and animal metabolism. And chemicals destroy the colloidal and living properties that hold soil together. It's difficult, no matter the sympathy I may feel toward farmers, or how many reassurances I hear about negligible numbers of waterfowl mortalities, to understand why poisonous chemicals should be allowed on publicly owned wildlife refuges.

Wendell Wood agrees. In correspondence on Oregon Natural Resource Council letter-head stationery, while discussing the extraordinary number of past management failures hinted at in the draft integrated pest management plan, Wood says, "We view the continued and sanctioned use of pesticides on Wildlife Refuges as but a symptom of the greater problem. Refuges must be managed for wildlife first."

Wood points out that this draft of the plan does "not even set goals for reducing pesticide use, let alone mandate reductions." And that, again quoting the draft plan, under the preferred alternative, "The number of approved chemicals might increase over the short and long terms." The ONRC, Wood says, is asking that the agencies managing the refuges "stop pesticide poisoning by requiring conversion of refuge agriculture to organic farming within five years," and that they "support gradual restoration of refuge farms to native marsh."

In regard to regional economics, Wood quotes the draft plan: "In the long term, it is assumed that the value of Refuge croplands would be recognized as some of the best in the nation. While the land's value would decrease for conventional growers, its pesticide-free status could improve its value for organic growers." Wood also emphasizes that the 210 leases on 22,000 acres of refuge farmlands were in the hands of only fifty-seven leaseholders, and that the lease-land revenue payments represented less than 1 percent of the budgets of Modoc and Siskiyou Counties in Northern California, and Klamath County in southern Oregon. The draft plan says the economic impact of a switch to organic farming would be "negligible to minor for the counties." Local economies would not be ruined.

The Tule Lake National Wildlife Refuge logged 196,544 recreational visitors in 1995, and the number of visitors (including more than 10,000 hunters) totaled some 164,000 on Lower Klamath. The draft integrated pest management plan tells us that "total expenditures were estimated at $700,400 for visitor recreation at Tule Lake NWR in fiscal year 1995. It is estimated that for every $1.00 spent at the Refuge, $1.50 is generated by recreational visitation." In short, the refuges can pay for themselves even if entirely dedicated to wildlife habitat, without lease-land farming.

It's the role of radical conservationist groups like the Oregon Natural Resource Council to establish limits. They draw lines in the sand. Cross them, they say, and we'll sue. They consistently do what they say they are going to do. Their existence constitutes a backboard for the rest of society to play against. The ONRC and Wendell Wood have declined a role in Klamath Basin environmental decision-making groups for a simple reason. They want to avoid being tempted to compromise through involvement with a group that is attempting to salvage both the local economy and the environment, rather than physical ecologies only. Which is ONRC's single concern. The Klamath Basin is lucky to have Wendell Wood. Not because he's necessarily correct, or incorrect, on any issue, but because his actions, those incessant lawsuits, force people to consider important concerns in public forums—in cafes, in the news-

Thurston and Sam Henzel, farmers, and their grain elevator straddling Highway 97, Worden, Oregon, 1998.

papers, on television, and ultimately, sadly, in court. Wendell Wood lives an adversarial life. It would not be anything I could stand, but he seems to consider his isolation in the community simply part of the price he is willing to pay in order to serve his purposes.

The basic quandary before the agencies and the national public is not so much whether pesticide use on the refuges is in the public interest (clearly, it's not), but whether the lease-land farming system itself should be continued.

Survival involves responding to change. Ranchers and farmers, after generations of living with the swings of climate and markets, know it better than anyone. But I couldn't bring myself to say that to Sam Henzel, whose family is legendary for hard work and smart dealings. Sam has seen a lot of the changes in the ways business is done in the Klamath Basin. He doesn't like what he's seen lately. He doesn't think he can change his ways of farming and stay in business. He's battling what he regards as both betrayal and senseless change.

On a quiet late September afternoon Tupper and I stopped to visit Henzel in his office, nearby to his big grain-shipping elevators in Worden, in the Lower Klamath Basin near the California border. The crops were harvested, and Henzel seemed to be in an expansive mood. He reminded me that the stories of his family and mine were much the same—determined, hard-working people who got a chance to break out new farmlands during the Great Depression, and made it pay.

Jack Liskey, Lower Klamath
Lake, Oregon, 1998. Liskey
brings up the end of his
seventieth spring cattle drive,
headed for the Liskey Ranch
adjacent to Lower Klamath
National Wildlife Refuge.

His father, Ben Henzel, and his uncle Dick Henzel started farming in the Tule Lake Basin in 1932. In 1948, in partnership with Dave and Dan Liskey, they incorporated Tulana Farms. After the Liskey brothers died in the 1950s, the Henzels kept Tulana Farms. In the 1960s they began developing farmland on the north end of Agency Lake. But the climate proved to be a few degrees too cold for barley or potatoes. In 1976, after a series of crop failures at Agency Lake, they sold Tulana Farms. Sam Henzel stayed in the farming business. With others in his family he bought the Tulana Farms properties in Lower Klamath and the elevator at Worden. Henzel has since made himself into an agribusiness leader, farming and brokering grain to the dairy and pleasure-horse trade and for export.

The Bureau of Reclamation, Henzel says, acts like it is ready to simply forget its promises to farmers. The tribes claim the water. What do the tribes want? Do they want to trade for land, in order to get their reservation back? Do they want to sell the water? What's going on? Henzel shakes his head. "The environment hasn't suffered that much," he says. "There's still plenty of birds. But now, there's this outsider awareness. We've got 3 million farmers left in the United States, and 40 million environmentalists." The next step, Henzel says, may be the condemnation of farmlands. "The government came in here with a plan, and farmers lived up to their side of the deal. They've done what they were supposed to do. Now they are being crowded out. What do people want? Turn the whole basin back into a swamp? If the public wants our lands they ought to pay a big price."

The second time I saw Sam Henzel was on a December afternoon, in what was the most elegant eating place in downtown Klamath Falls when I was a boy, the Pelican Cafe, where

Luther Horsley and daughter,
Jessica, Midland, Oregon,
1998.

my mother used to go for luncheons with her friends. The main item on the menu these days is pizza. The business offices of the Warner Valley Livestock Company, the corporation that owned and managed properties my family had accumulated, used to be just upstairs from the Pelican Cafe, in the Williams Building, which was built in the early days by Buck Williams, who established the Yamsi Ranch. Old-time connections everywhere. Sam was there with Jack Liskey and Luther Horsley, large-scale farmers in Lower Klamath. The three of them are the directors of the Lower Klamath Drainage District. They had met that morning to contemplate another lawsuit by the ONRC.

Sam Henzel is, in a major way, one of the lease-land farmers on the wildlife refuges. The federal government, he told me, has for decades encouraged him to pursue lease-land farming. He has a considerable amount of money invested in equipment. A lot of his family story turns around such farming. He's spent his life on the intricacies of making it pay. Sam gave me a very direct look and asked what I'd do if I was trying to deal with their problems. Absurdly, I tried to answer. "Don't let them isolate you." Sounded stupid at the time, still does. But it turns out to be sort of what I meant. Don't let the processes of community be ultimately torn apart. Don't let your anger lead you into isolation.

There are other ways to farm. That's what I didn't have the guts to say. Might be a very good idea, at this stage in the game, to start checking them out. Sam Henzel, I think, knows as well as anyone that chemical-based agriculture is widely understood as a threat to the environment and to national health standards. But for the next few years he's got a chance to win in court, and hold trouble at bay. I think he feels coerced, if he wants to stay in business, to try.

My sympathy for Sam Henzel is profound, partly because in him I see a life I could have lived. My family got out of ranching in the late 1960s. I thought of taking my resources and trying to buy my way back in. But I didn't have the money, and I had other fish to fry. I went off to another life. If not for those circumstances I might be fighting Sam Henzel's battles with him, hiring lawyers and trying to fend off change. I can feel as betrayed as the next man, and be as angry and as stubborn. But I probably would have bagged the enterprise. My father told me to avoid spending time on things you hate, like legal entanglements. I wouldn't be willing to spend my life on them. I wonder if Sam is. Fifty percent of his time, Henzel says, is spent on trying to stay in business, working with lawyers. Which doesn't leave much for the pleasures of farming. We have only so much future. It makes the going a lot easier to take if we love what's on the horizon every morning. One sure thing: agriculturalists in the Klamath Basin, until they learn to rethink their ways of doing business, are going to spend more and more on lawyers.

The draft integrated pest management plan, which came out in July 1998, signals the beginning of a new era in the use of pesticides on lease lands in refuges, the beginning of a new relationship between farmers on the lease lands and the agencies in charge of the refuges.

Growers like Henzel want to continue farming as they have for decades. But national conservationist sentiments are demanding to be recognized, insisting that farmers on the refuges' lease lands be at least required to farm without chemicals, in an entirely organic fashion. That political fact of life is inherent everywhere in the *Environmental Assessment*.

Near Knight's Landing in the Sacramento Valley, I talked to a man who was farming organically on 2,000 acres. He claimed to be making more money than ever: "They're paying a big premium for organic. We couldn't survive in any other way." The Fetzer winery in Northern California is largely organic. They're getting a premium for their products, a jump start on the future. And there's a folk story about the vast Gallo wineries. The old man who owned the company announced that they would have to start raising grapes organically. A foreman objected, "We can't do that." The old man smiled a sweet smile, and said, "Oh, yes, I think we can." And they did, whether that story is true or not. And they prosper. "There's nothing so bad," Sam Henzel says, "about the status quo." As if he were talking about something written in stone.

At the end of April 1998, Tupper and I visited John Walker, a native of Merrill who farms around 1,300 acres. We read in the newspaper that he used garlic as a pesticide on 115 acres of Tule Lake land in 1997, and that he was calling the trial a success. Only 10 percent of his potatoes had been damaged by pests. Walker found out about garlic in a vegetable grower's handbook, and called around to growers in California and Texas to see if it worked. "They were using it on cotton," he said.

Walker used garlic and Vapam, a conventional chemical pesticide, side by side. Results were about the same. Garlic also repels leafhoppers, armyworms, thrips, and mice. And it's far cheaper than chemicals. "Farmers are challenged," Walker said. "If we're going to stay

William Walker and John Walker, Merrill, Oregon, 1998. The Walkers are experimenting with garlic and fish oil, instead of the customary chemical pesticides, to control pests on their potato farm.

in row crops on the Tule Lake lease lands we've got to show people that we're expanding our horizons. We've got to find something that works."

At the end of August 1998 I called to see how the second year of garlic treatment had worked out. "We've dug about 10 acres so far," he said. "No bugs. Seems like it worked." By spring of 1999 the verdict was "It helps."

Let's hope it does. Makes you wonder, where were agricultural scientists when farmers in California and Texas were having success with garlic as a pesticide? Why weren't there any field trials on the Tule Lake lease lands?

Summer thunderstorm,
Wood River, Oregon.

11

WETLANDS

A widely agreed-upon, short-term remedy for Klamath Basin watershed problems is a plan to redevelop wetlands. It's endorsed by conservationists and farmers and ranchers. Wetlands filter drainage water coming off farm- and ranch lands upstream, provide habitat for waterfowl, spawning grounds for endangered fish, and late-season upstream storage for irrigators. Win, win, win. But the working out is never so simple.

North of Klamath Lake, there's a reach of grazing meadows—cut by sod-banked fishing rivers, the Sprague, the Williamson, and the Wood, and centered on the tiny country town of Fort Klamath—that constitute one of the most appealing landscapes in the American West. Fertile, framed by aspen groves, it looks to have once been a paradise of hunting animals like mule deer and elk. If the truly rich with their enormous invulnerabilities and funds ever decide to buy into the Klamath country, the way they have bought up parts of Montana, where I live, they'll probably start around the Fort. In the meantime, as it has been for decades, Fort Klamath is grazing country. About 40,000 acres support 40,000 cows and calves for the summer, some 240,000 animal-unit months.

The Williamson River, the Sprague, and the Wood carry an enormous load of livestock waste into Klamath Lake. Polluting prime trout habitat on the way, they feed nutrients to processes in the lake that result in a huge annual bloom of blue-green algae, which then dies and settles. Bacteria decompose the algae and, as they do, deplete oxygen levels in the lake, which becomes both acidic and hypoxic, unlivable for fish (these same processes, because of nitrogen and various other nutrients from the Mississippi River system, have led to the formation of a seven-thousand-square-mile "dead zone" in the seawaters of the Gulf of Mexico off Louisiana). The summer drawdown from the lake, which provides water for irrigators, heightens the problem. Reaches of the lake in late summer in dry years are reduced to mudflats. The shores are littered with decaying fish. Those that survive are mainly the ones that migrate up into the streams. Water from the basin, thick with sediment, flows into the Klamath River. Oxygen levels in the Klamath River in 1986, between Lake Ewauna and Keno, fell to near zero, killing thousands of fish. Responding to sportfishers and the commercial fishing industry and the various tribes, Congress created the Klamath Basin Fish-

"Like winds and sunsets, wild things were taken for granted
until progress began to do away with them. Now we face
the question of whether a still higher 'standard of living'
is worth its cost in things natural, wild, and free."

eries Restoration Task Force and gave them the task of developing a salmon recovery plan. Farmers in the basin, fearful of losing irrigation water, didn't cooperate. After years of interest-group infighting, the process seems stalled.

That same year, 1986, the Klamath tribes asked the U.S. Fish and Wildlife Service to protect two species of fish they regard as culturally valuable, the *qapdo* (pronounced *kuptu*) and *c'wam* (pronounced *ch-wam*). These fish, also known as shortnose and Lost River suckers, exist only in the Klamath Basin. In 1988 the agency listed both species as endangered. Reclamation was forced to ensure water in habitat where the suckers spawned. Which meant less water for irrigators. Many were furious. But the trouble was just beginning. By 1991 Reclamation had not yet begun work on a plan to ensure the recovery of the suckers. A lawsuit by the ONRC asked that Reclamation be required to consult with federal biologists on matters having to do with the welfare of the suckers. It was, environmentalists say, a way of "requiring them to do their job."

The Klamath Basin Water Users, an alliance of irrigation districts, farm supply companies, and Klamath Basin business leaders, responded by hiring scientists and lawyers. Serious water wars in the Klamath Basin were under way.

All these problems were exacerbated in 1992 by one of the severe drouths connected to so-called El Niño events in the Pacific. Extreme habitat problems in the Klamath River system caused the Pacific Fisheries Management Council to cut the number of salmon that could be harvested in the ocean. The Department of Interior, under pressure from downstream interests, ordered Reclamation to release more water for the salmon into the Klamath River. The Bureau of Reclamation, for the first time since the formation of the district, had to restrict and in some cases cut off water to irrigators in the lower end of the basin, affecting around 70,000 acres of cropland. The Bureau, in order to avoid having to cut irrigators even more, drained Clear Lake Reservoir to the lowest levels ever, a move considered harmful to a native population of pelicans. Efforts that winter by the Bureau to review the allocation process didn't get far. "There was a heavy snowpack in 1993," the head of the Bureau said, "and the farmers were in denial."

Nineteen ninety-four was another drouth year. The Bureau cut water to irrigators a second time, ultimately to all irrigators for periods ranging from two to six weeks. As the head of the Bureau said, "Some were just enraged."

The fury of farmers on lands served by the enormous run of irrigation projects developed by the Bureau of Reclamation was understandable. They had been promised all the water they could use. No one imagined the supply would ever run short.

Dr. Karl Wenner and Alice
Kilham, Hank's Marsh,
Upper Klamath Lake,
Oregon, 1998. These two
were the original cochairs of
the Hatfield Klamath Basin
Working Group.

In the meantime, back at Fort Klamath, up toward the head of the watershed, under pressure from environmental groups like Oregon Trout, ranchers voluntarily built fish ladders around irrigation dams and fenced off streamsides. While those efforts were admirable, they were not going to cure the core problem, animal waste in the watershed.

In response to this thicket of interrelated troubles, the Oregon senator Mark Hatfield (since retired) held a hearing in Klamath Falls on July 6, 1994. Hatfield felt that the testimony of local citizens at that hearing offered ample evidence of the desire and willingness of the community to resolve economic and environmental issues at the basin level. He appointed twenty-seven people, representing public and private interests, to a consortium called the Hatfield Klamath Basin Working Group.

Hatfield asked them to develop projects focused on ecosystem restoration, economic stability, and the reduction of drouth impacts, and promised his support and help in implementing those projects. The Working Group first met on April 6, 1995, and on May 17 it sent a short list of projects to Hatfield for inclusion in the Fiscal Year 1996 Federal Budget. Senator Hatfield obtained $3,500,000 for the purchase of 4,700 acres of former Tulana Farms land at the mouth of the Williamson River and $725,000 for use by the U.S. Fish and Wildlife Service in riparian restoration. Working Group proposals for fiscal year 1997 resulted in $5,500,000 for wetlands restoration on the Tulana Farms land, and $500,000 for restoration of wetlands on property purchased in 1994 by the Bureau of Land Management at the mouth of the Wood River.

Bald eagle,
Williamson River
delta, Oregon.

Jim Carpenter took some hours away from his Cell Tech duties and drove Tupper and Madeleine and me to sad old polluted Lake Ewauna on the edge of downtown Klamath Falls. Sunken timbers left over from its log-pond days are reputed to lie one on top of the other to a depth of fifty feet, decaying into the nutrient overload that feeds into the Klamath River. Timber-milling buildings along the edge of the lake, the old Modoc Lumber Company, have been torn down, the equipment allegedly shipped to Siberia, leaving 400 acres for development. Carpenter hopes some of that development, along with cobblestone streets and upscale shops, will be wetlands.

The idea, Carpenter said, is to ring the lake with marshes that will also function as downtown city parks. Living in a city with downtown parks helps citizens feel positive about the possibility of a good life where they live. Which in turn drives economic activity. Wetlands are good for nature, and economically sensible, feasible, and good for community. No negatives.

The next day Carpenter drove us to the north end of Klamath Lake, to the delta of the Williamson River, for a look at the 4,700 acres formerly drained and farmed by Tulana Farms. In July 1996, with the intention of returning the entire acreage to wetlands, the Nature Conservancy had bought the property. But farmers protested that there was no other "clean" ground in the Klamath Basin for the production of seed potatoes, so Nature Conservancy administrators agreed to continued farming on 1,150 acres. They plan to return 3,650 acres to permanent wetlands. The plan was endorsed by the Klamath tribes, and restoration work was funded at the request of the Hatfield Klamath Basin Working Group. But others saw the final deal as an instance of rolling over when confronted with the economic power of regional agribusiness. The decision-making, it was said, had been undemocratic, involving secret meetings. To give decision makers credit, it's often impossible to do business with private owners if details of the negotiations are going to make the newspapers. And the wetlands, in any event, are a very good idea.

In 1994 the Bureau of Land Management acquired the Wood River Ranch on Agency Lake, a northern arm of Klamath Lake, planning to reestablish wetlands at the mouth of Wood River and restore the river to its traditional channel in old stream meanders. Wedge Watkins, a longtime Bureau of Land Management employee supervising the restoration, had heavy equipment at work rebuilding dikes. "When they drained this place," he says, "the surface subsided. We're three or four feet below the lake surface. So we're stuck with these dikes for a long time." A big pumping plant, to move water in and out, was already in place. Artifice covering artifice, imitating the natural.

Northern pintail, female preening, Williamson River delta, Oregon.

Wedge Watkins gazed off toward the beauties of the Wood River Valley, aspen groves and winding watercourses, and meadows thick with grazing cattle. "With so much livestock upstream," he said, "we have to absorb about the equivalent of 250,000 people dumping their sewage into this watershed." The marsh will work as a water filter, a spawning ground, and as upstream storage for late-season irrigation in the lower basin. A lot of problems addressed with one redeveloped marshland. But, again, people had complaints about the way the property was acquired, in a land trade—the Wood River marshes for 520 acres of old-growth forest. The federal government, it was said, should have simply bought the properties. For sure, if the old growth is cut, it will be a sad loss in territory where there was once so much so-called virgin timber.

During the winter of 1997–98, for an estimated cost of $5 million, the 7,123-acre Agency Lake Ranch, on the shore of Agency Lake, was bought by the Trust for Public Lands and

its control given over to the Bureau of Reclamation (it will be purchased by the federal government). The land is to be flooded, enabling the Bureau to store around 15,000 acre-feet of water behind existing dikes, and 40,000 acre-feet after the dike system is built up.

It's hoped that these wetlands will provide water to cover shortages in the basin in all but the driest years (there are people who claim that this, given evaporation rates of around 4 acre-feet per year, is nonsense). Summer nutrient loading in Klamath Lake will in any event be reduced by removal of some eight thousand grazing livestock. And as water is released it will be filtered through marshlands. Some of the toxic microcystin algae will be filtered out.

These projects are presently thought of as major successes. They have brought a wide range of diverse economic and environmental interests into previously unheard-of working partnerships, and waterbirds will throng to the remade marshes.

Redhead, female and brood, Wood River, Oregon.

Long-billed dowitchers,

Wood River,

Oregon.

American avocet,

Wood River,

Oregon.

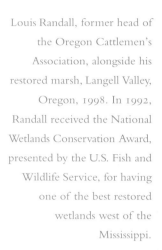

Louis Randall, former head of
the Oregon Cattlemen's
Association, alongside his
restored marsh, Langell Valley,
Oregon, 1998. In 1992,
Randall received the National
Wetlands Conservation Award,
presented by the U.S. Fish and
Wildlife Service, for having
one of the best restored
wetlands west of the
Mississippi.

Jim Hainline took Madeleine and Tupper and me out to have lunch with Louis Randall and
his wife, Maren, at their Langell Valley home in the Lost River drainage, near the place where
wetlands reclamation in the Klamath Basin got under way in 1868, as the Langell family settled in. (It's also the setting for a Zane Grey novel called *The Forlorn River*.)

Randall created 800 acres of private wetlands under a conservation easement, and he pro-
poses 300 more, work carried out for the common good, with the help of federal experts
for sure, but for their own and the common good. When I asked how far he'd go with re-
creating marshlands, Randall said, "Just as soon put the whole thing in." In the days before
the Lost River channel was dredged, it was all wetlands. "We cut hay on the high ground,"
Randall said. "Then we broke it up. Plowed the whole summer of 1945. Put in oats in 1946.
For forty years we farmed it, but it was marginal grain land." Randall says he got the idea
of creating marshes from duck hunters who came back year after year for the fall shooting
in his fields. Now, he said, he's making more off the hunting leases than he ever did with
grain. And it's easy. "Keep it wet," he said, "and let the tules grow."

Louis Randall is in his seventies and very well regarded in Oregon, a prosperous man (his
wife, Maren, served us lunch beside their enclosed swimming pool) and a former head of
the Oregon Cattleman's Association. If anybody had a chance to be locked into traditional
ranching, Louis Randall is the man. But, he said, "we can't go back. We have to go forward." With the marshlands, he's making money, and he's proud of himself for working
to leave things as alive as he found them when he was young.

A few days later, Jim Hainline took Madeleine and Tupper and me to visit with a rancher named Dan Byrne, who comes from a longtime ranching family. Byrne runs cows on private and federally owned highland country, a lot of it rocky juniper flats east of the Clear Lake National Wildlife Refuge.

    Cowmen using public lands, like those managed by the Forest Service and the Bureau of Land Management in Klamath County, face image problems that seem to be getting worse. Grazing fees, set in Washington, D.C., with western Congressmembers looking on, are often well below market rates. Ranchers, as seen by the public, are getting huge subsidies. Cows eat feed that could be used by overwintering wildlife. They trash riparian zones and pollute recreation areas. Cows, no matter what livestock producers say, are more and more unpopular with the national public. For decades, livestock producers have denied their problems, putting out a line of talk that sells in their meetings and in ranch land cafes. But the general public isn't buying it. The rancher's fund of good will in the nation at large has

Greater white-fronted geese, Lost River wetlands, Langell Valley, Oregon.

Dan Byrne, Boles Creek,
California, 1998. Byrne
uses solar technology
to control livestock in his
effort to improve streams
and riparian areas.

been seriously eroded. It can only be restored through some national public-lands policy revamping. And by the work of ranchers who use the rangelands.

Dan Byrne, with bureaucrats from the Forest Service and the U.S. Fish and Wildlife Service running interference, is turning things around on his operation. Old fences, built in the 1930s by the Civilian Conservation Corps, were down, and cattle were in creek bottoms and wetlands used by wildlife. Byrne built a lot of new fence, guaranteeing it would be maintained; he developed stock water from wells powered by solar energy, cleared brush and juniper, and reseeded grasslands. Each step had to be worked out in ways specific to the place, by people who understood local conditions. Room for failure, for learning, was built into the management system. One problem with public-lands management is the unceasing public demand for immediate unconditional success. Management ought to be a monitored but flexible process, subject to failure like any human work, based on the best science but able to respond to changing annual and seasonal conditions.

"Generating community trust," Byrne said, "between ranchers and bureaucrats and the public, is the key. If some solutions don't work out, others will. If we can learn to trust the people involved, we're on our way to common ground, to getting down to work. There's no reason wildlife and cattle can't exist together." We couldn't, because of muddy roads, get out to see his rangeland. We spent a morning talking and looking at before and after photographs of scablands transformed into thick stands of grass, and new wells, and fenced springs, projects good for both wildlife and grazing. "It was frustrating, and a lot of hard work," Byrne said. "And it cost money. But we're ready for the future."

Jim Hainline keeps on promoting the welfare of agricultural communities. By the summer of 1998 he'd brought together a group of ranchers on the upper Williamson River—John Hyde and Clinton Basey among them—to begin talking to ecological scientists and thinking about practical ways to improve watershed conditions. Hainline could point to models like the turnaround Linda Rexroat has worked out on Sycan Marsh. The ranchers and conservationists are talking to one another in reasoning ways. Sensible talk, rather than rhetoric.

Not all the basin problems involving wetlands and agriculture are so solvable. Sumps in the Tule Lake refuge are huge ponds where irrigation water drained off farmlands is stored until it's pumped over into Lower Klamath. The Kuchel Act locks in 13,000 acres as sump land, defining them as wildlife habitat. But waterbird numbers are way down in the Tule Lake refuge, and have been for decades. The problem, Jim Hainline told me as we drove the levee banks, is habitat. Over decades the sumps silted in at a rate of around an inch every

Sage grouse,
Clear Lake,
California.

Pronghorn young,
Clear Lake Hills,
California.

Great Basin wild rye,
Horse Mountain,
California.

two years. Some have lost fourteen feet in depth. They tend to be shallow, muddy lakes or are overgrown with vegetation. Waterbirds prefer open water mixed with islands of marshland. Water quality problems—high pH, low dissolved oxygen, high temperatures, and unionized ammonia—are also endemic. And, despite local efforts to deny the likelihood, so long as chemical agents are used to fertilize, kill weeds, and control diseases and other pests on adjacent farmlands, there's a chance water in the sumps may be chemically contaminated. The sumps are also poor habitat for fish. The U.S. Fish and Wildlife Service's 1998 draft integrated pest management plan says, "The artificial character of the sumps and the poor environmental quality have allowed the sucker population to approach collapse within the Tule Lake Refuge area." They're talking about endangered suckers whose welfare is of intense concern to the Klamath Indians, who have prior rights to the use of this water. They're talking about problems that could lead to courtroom confrontations. So. Not many birds, dying fish. But lots of first-rate farming. Not your ideal wildlife refuge.

A proposed cure for the decrease in waterfowl numbers at Tule Lake, and for water quality problems in general, is "sump rotation." The sumps would be dried up, plowed, farmed as lease land, and an equal amount of former lease land would be flooded, turned into sump land, in hopes of restoring habitat for suckers and waterbirds. The farmers involved would be burdened with breaking out new land, a difficult and expensive proposition. I asked Jim Hainline why farmers would be interested. "They think it's their only chance to keep farming the lease lands. They want to show that farming and wetlands can work in a partnership. They think it's that or lose the lease-lands program altogether."

Hainline took me to visit Marshall Staunton, whose family has been farming in the Tule Lake country since his grandfather came from the East to homestead there in 1929. The Staunton family partnership raises wheat, barley, onions, and potatoes on 2,200 acres of private land. They also farm rented land and Tule Lake lease land.

I'd met Marshall Staunton months before, at a meeting of watershed scientists in Yreka, California, when he'd grinned and introduced himself as a "green farmer." What he meant by that, I came to realize, was that he was an on-the-ground farmer who knew that he faced environmental problems. And that he was trying to figure out solutions. Many farmers and ranchers in the Klamath Basin were in belligerent denial. Staunton was enthusiastic about the idea of farming the sumps. "We can show the world that wildlife and development are compatible," he said. "That would be a beginning." Indeed it would.

But lately the sump rotation project is on hold. Another round of research seems indicated. Farming in the sumps might stir up waterfowl disease agents. Flooding longtime farm ground might exacerbate problems with avian botulism. Water in new sumps might become overloaded with nitrogen and phosphorous (fertilizer residues) released from old farm ground, and the new sumps might become hypotrophic. Sump rotation looks increasingly like a quick fix that won't fix anything in the long run, which may cause as much or more trouble than it could possibly cure. The real cure, according to the ONRC, would be marsh restoration of the sort going on around the fringes of Klamath Lake, not any Band-Aid "sump restorations" of the sort proposed by the Fish and Wildlife Service. Forget the lease-land farming.

What about the farmers, led for generations by Reclamation and Fish and Wildlife Service bureaucrats, who built lives and communities around farming land they don't own, irrigating with water they don't own? Do we as a nation owe them anything? Or have we given them enough already? "We've got to figure something out," Marshall Staunton told me. "Farmers are down to hiring lawyers. That's all they can think of. They're settling into a siege mentality."

Voices begin to accumulate. Farmers and ranchers wonder, "What's wrong with the status quo?" Others say, "If we want to survive, we have to make some changes." Wetland redevelopment is clearly a good thing. But many locals have serious concerns as to whether these moves are sufficient to ensure the long-term integrity of the system. It's easy to say wetlands are just extemporizing, Band-Aid solutions designed to quiet public relations turmoil. "Those boys at the Bureau," a man told me, "are just trying to glue the system together until they can retire." Jim Kerns, a second-generation Klamath Falls resident and dealer in irrigation systems, has for years been saying that the only long-term solution for Klamath Basin water problems lies in deep upstream storage. Kerns advocates building two high dams. The first, at Aspen Lake, on the west side of Klamath Lake, would be 120 feet high and able to store 750,000 acre-feet. The second, in Boundary Canyon on the Lost River just downstream from Clear Lake, would be 116 feet high and able to store 40,000 acre-feet (it would dry up one lobe of Clear Lake). Kerns says this is necessary for two reasons, both having to do with the wide rainfall variations in wet and dry years. Two million acre-feet of water flow down the Klamath River in wet years, 400,000 acre-feet in dry years.

Dave Mauser and Marshall
Staunton, Tulelake, California,
1998. Mauser, a biologist for
the U.S. Fish and Wildlife
Service, and Staunton, a
farmer leasing federal lands,
worked to implement a sump
rotation plan intended to
allow farming to continue
on refuge lands.

Downstream salmon recovery needs at least 700,000 acre-feet per year. It's crazy, Kerns says, to let all that water get away in wet years. Shallow storage, he says, won't do. Stored water in the Klamath Basin evaporates at a rate of three-tenths of an inch per day, or 4 acre-feet per year. Water stored to a depth of 4 feet, as in wetlands being re-created along the shores of Klamath Lake, Kerns points out, leaves you with a mudflat the next spring.

But there are grave objections to Kerns's plan. The first is the cost, around $200 million for the dams (against $5 million for the Agency Lake Ranch). And wetlands at Aspen Lake would be inundated. And Boundary Canyon, according to what I've heard from non-Indian sources, is thick with archeological sites. Jim Kerns's high-dam plan might have been embraced in the West of a few decades back, but the time when it could have been sold to a national public seems to have come and gone. Imagine the lawsuits.

Everything incessantly changes. Survival depends on being willing and able to rethink techniques and technologies, strategies. Otherwise the international economic system will be quite willing to do business without us. People in the Klamath Basin are unlikely to find absolute solutions to their watershed problems, but their efforts to restore ecologies are steps toward enduring.

Sandhill cranes,
Klamath Marsh,
Oregon.

12

NEIGHBORHOODS

The bright fire in overcast December twilight, children dancing around, throwing junk wood into the flames, announced ancient civilities, family and light, warmth. These looked to be people who valued ceremony. And they were young, child-rearing people. We'd found Mike Connelly's place south of Bonanza, in Langell Valley, well up in the Lost River drainage among runs of manicured hay land between juniper ridges, dairy farms, small livestock outfits with grazing permits on forestlands to the east, barns, and tight country homes, another version of heartland America.

Tupper and Madeleine and I had heard lots of points of view, spoken with urgency by people with personal, ideological, and financial interests in the drama playing out in the Klamath Basin. How to tell this mix of personal and political stories without betraying anyone, including myself? I was glad to leave my notebook in Tupper's Land Rover, mix with the children and barking dogs, and crack open a can of Budweiser.

The children, long-haired Anna, and Reno, maybe three, his hair brush-cut like his father's, were quite overwhelmingly beautiful. Dancing near the flames, they flirted, touching us, going shy before touching us again. No one pretended that they should control themselves. "Some mornings, in the spring," Mike Connelly said, "there's sandhill cranes dancing on that meadow." This was a sort of private message. Sandhill cranes are important to me, presences from my childhood in Warner Valley, and Connelly knew it. We were at that stage between people meeting one another called exchanging credentials. Connelly was saying something to the effect that he understood the value of great birds at their courtship dances in your own meadows, and that he was raising his children to understand. Connelly and his friend, Shawn Gillihan, are young married men who came to the Klamath country, after some educational wandering, from the upscale, wine-growing Napa Valley. They are intellectuals (they'll hate me for that one) who seem to have decided to invest their lives in the processes of particular communities. "Me and the kids," Mike said, "try to come out here every few nights and burn some wood." He was making a point in favor of rituals, and a secure, established emotional life, the need to take deliberate care, of your place and your people.

Sandy and Mike Connelly with their children, Reno and Anna Mitra, northern foot of Bryant Mountain, Oregon, 1998. "There's lots we don't know about how this river does and doesn't work," says Mike. "But there's one thing we're damn sure of: no irrigation, no Connellys."

People like me, we fled, and did our thinking at a distance. Connelly had come to the Klamath country determined to see his thoughts about community work out in life, not just in his head. Connelly owns 366 acres of deeded hay land and leases 2,000 acres of private and Bureau of Land Management grazing land. He runs a hundred registered Hereford cows. It's a small operation in western terms. After time working for the Stag's Leap Winery in Napa, Connelly got an American studies degree from the University of California at Davis, where he encountered people like the poet Gary Snyder. Then he took a master's degree from the University of Wyoming. During that time he was sorting out thoughts about community and the environment, and the way taking care of one implies taking care of the other.

"I got disgusted with intellectual environmentalists. Nature to them is like some lover they pick up in a bar. An attractive abstraction but not somebody you'd want to live with. They aren't willing to wake up in the boondocks for the rest of their lives. For farmers, it's different, like being married, hell or high water, every morning, all day, for life.

"Sounds judgmental," he said, "but I think farmers and ranchers have an adult relationship with the world. That's what I want." Yes, I thought, if he was saying most people don't have an adult relationship to their surroundings, it did in fact sound judgmental. But it also sounded like somebody trying to say what he meant. Mike and Shawn cooked, Mike's wife, Sandy, came home from work as a medical assistant in two small local clinics, and all of us sipped shots of single-malt Scotch. The thick, center-cut pork chops and light salad seemed

Jim Hainline, chief biologist
of the Klamath Basin
National Wildlife Refuge
Complex, at Butte Valley
Airport, Butte Valley,
California, 1998.

perfect, and so did the wines. "Napa Valley was overrun by tourists," Mike said. "I couldn't stand it. So here we are."

Connelly's community work centers on the Clover Leaf Watershed Council, a volunteer group trying to develop consensus solutions to problems along a reach of the Lost River they think of as being in the neighborhood. "It goes slowly, trying to figure out what consensus means," Connelly said. "We're all fighting wars in our heads."

Watershed working groups are a phenomenon cropping up among farmers and ranchers in the Flathead Valley of Montana, and urban citizens in Ann Arbor along the Huron River. Irrevocably shared watershed troubles are driving citizens to form de facto political entities dedicated to solving problems. Citizens are working to transcend political ideologies and take responsibility for the neighborhood ecologies that are the basis for their regional economy.

There's a common rap on agency people who stay too long in one place. They bond to communities where they are living and forget their commitment to larger goals. Jim Hainline has found his home and work in the Klamath Basin, and he admits he's wedded to furthering the well-being of Klamath farmers and communities.

When Louis Randall wanted to start developing a private wetland, he encountered a lot of bureaucracy. You can't, these days, even on your own land, just rework water flow patterns. You have to think of downstream users. There are reams of paperwork. Jim Hainline helped Randall think through the project, and saw him through the paperwork. Same thing for Dan Byrne, when he was faced with revamping his grazing system. Both men admit that without Hainline they might have given up.

The results are good work—good for the people who did the work, their families, the future of agriculture in the basin, and for local ecologies—the result of a practical relationship, based on trust and respect, between a bureaucrat and a couple of ranchers. Hainline has invented a role for himself. He's an advocate for both agricultural people and the environment. We ought to insist there be federal agency job descriptions based on Hainline's career. People coming out of agricultural schools and wildlife biology programs might aspire to such work. It would be a noble calling. Western on-the-ground people might find their relationships with the bureaucracies vastly improved. People in the public lands of the West might be a lot closer to forming functional watershed communities, a hell of a lot happier, and better off economically.

Building trust, helping landowners design watershed reclamation projects, helping with the paperwork, working as an ombudsman, seeing them through. The Klamath Basin is lucky to have citizens like Hainline and Jim Carpenter and Wendell Wood, Louis Randall and Jeff Mitchell, people who often don't share much but a determination to solve problems. They're stuck with one another and are recognizing and attempting to resolve their differences.

Maybe the brightest sign of hope in the Klamath Basin lies with the younger citizens who seem so intent on preserving their communities—like Linda Rexroat and Becky Hatfield-Hyde, Marshall Staunton and Mike Connelly. It's easy to imagine the word out on E-mail: you could invest your life and energy in the Klamath Basin with some good chance of having a positive effect.

MANAGING THE COMMONS: CONSENSUS

Generation after generation of native people in the Klamath country hunted on the timbered ridgelines, went to the berrying grounds and *wokas* beds, snared waterbirds in the marshes where they congregated, and fished for suckers and salmon in the streams and lakes. Theirs was once the common human situation. Territories lived in by hunting and gathering peoples, to a varying but considerable degree, constituted a seemingly inexhaustible commons to be harvested by everyone.

The natural commons still to some degree exists. Clean air over the distances of the Grand Canyon, or the look of clouds on a wintery morning over Mount Shasta, which we do not think of as owned, are also part of our commons. And there's a humanmade commons. Both wildlife refuges and courthouses are part of the commons. And our common possessions are not limited to items that are fixed and defined or even always namable. Concern for the dying and the newborn, and joy in someone's ability to make good soup or bread or wine, are all part of our commons.

Ownership, private or common, can be both liberating and an entrapment. Our most valued powers, and our unavoidable and insistent responsibilities, personal and political, often proceed from ownership. This is particularly true of common ownership. Aristotle said, "What is common to the greatest number has the least care bestowed upon it. Everyone thinks chiefly of his own, hardly at all of the common interest." Hobbes's parable of human beings in a state of nature, seeking their own good, who end up fighting one another, is a prototype of what has been called "the tragedy of the commons." H. Scott Gordon wrote in 1954, talking about the idea of the commons, that "everybody's property is nobody's property. Wealth that is free for all is valued by no one, because he who is foolhardy enough to wait for its proper time of use will only find that it has been taken by another." In 1968 Garrett Hardin defined "the tragedy of the commons." He asked the reader to imagine a pasture "open to all." People suffered when it was overgrazed. Although each herder received direct benefits only from his own herd, the costs of overgrazing were shared. "Therein is the tragedy," said Hardin. "Each man is locked into a system that compels him to increase his herd without limit—in a world that is limited. Ruin is the destruction toward which all men rush, each pursuing his own best interest in a society that believes in the freedom of the commons."

Hardin suggested that only "mutual coercion mutually agreed upon" could restrain people from destroying the resources human life depends on. To save the future of the species, many immediate wants would have to be denied. Coercive episodes, people kicked out of places which had sustained their clans and families for generations, of the kind that took place when the commons in England was privatized in the nineteenth century, are likely to occur. But that, Hardin wrote, "is preferable to total ruin."

Hardin's definition of the problems involved in managing the commons resonated in thinking about public policy through the 1970s. But while all creatures are driven to succeed, we know, there are many definitions of success. Selfishness, the problem of "free riders" that Hardin believed would inevitably lead to the "tragedy of the commons," is a result of our desire to care for and perpetuate ourselves and our progeny. It's a consistent human response to life, but it can play out in more complex ways than Hardin seems to have imagined, for instance in systems of generosity. Cultures are often indifferent to the well-being of outsiders but generous to an extreme degree within the society.

Most of us who came of age in the American West were brought up in an acquisitive and individualistic, which is to say adversarial and survival-oriented, society. I once heard a man say that the rules for life he learned in west Texas could be summed up as "Take care of your own Goddamned self." But many of us were also brought up in locally generous societies. We're accustomed to putting our personal desires aside and acting for the good of others. We understand that such actions are ultimately good for us and the people we revere. Most of us want to believe we live in a society where kindness and humane generosity is ordinary, and we do believe it, most of the time. We act on that belief. Otherwise, we'd be in an incessant war zone. (Examples of what can happen if such belief breaks down surround us, as in Bosnia or Rwanda or Ireland or the Near East.) We run into generosity everywhere; acts of kindness grow wild, like roses in the fence lines.

Aristotle, Hobbes, and Garrett Hardin told us stories that they took to be universal. But cultures evolve. Ideas of useful economic and political conduct are contingent and can be rethought. Laws evolve in response to challenges. Laws are an organizing story we tell ourselves as we order our lives. People use law, as Clifford Geertz wrote, to "orient themselves in a world otherwise opaque." We are reasonable; we rethink our theories; we make new laws.

Users of the commons are not tragically driven to selfishness by their inherent natures, but rather motivated by cultural stories of who they are and how they are supposed to proceed, which are embodied in their customs and laws. Traditional native cultures in the Klamath Basin managed their common resources well enough, in part because they were small populations and the *wokas* fields and waterbirds were inexhaustibly abundant, but also because they were aware that they'd better take care of what they had because it was all they had. Communal ownership, to them, was commonplace. Their responsibilities were obvious. So are ours.

Responsibilities always constitute a limitation on freedom. Our highways are a commons. We don't get to drive when we're drunk. Common interest communities—small and local inside the regional and the national, the global, one talking to the other in straightforward ways, negotiating within frameworks of widely accepted democratic rules—equal about as much freedom as we are likely to realize inside the restraints of civilized life.

Our world can more and more accurately be defined as a set of international common resources—seas and rain forests, the ozone layer and gene pools and human communities, all woven into one another. The earthly biosystem, and the rest of our estate, concepts like order and peacefulness within systems of constraint and freedom, are a common pool of resources, and our responsibility. Societies with a history of caring for their share of things tend to be (1) stable communities, with (2) a shared past and the expectation of a shared future, and (3) a system of norms that includes the reputation of members for keeping promises, honest dealing, and reliability. These societies also have (4) a willingness to revise their rules in order to endure, (5) a system by which the owners of common resources (ideally the entire society) collectively monitor their use, and (6) ways of enforcing their rules.

But most important, they have a coherent vision of themselves as a society. They know what they want. Sensible plans for the future are difficult to develop in a community that doesn't know, or acknowledge, what it values. Citizens in the Klamath Basin, in this time of transition, are driven to work out such a vision of themselves, for themselves. This working out is complicated by the fact that they're simultaneously trying to refine a system of governance for the watershed commons they so clearly inhabit together.

A promisingly democratic forum for resolving such questions involves what is called consensus decision making—getting most people in the community to agree on what they want. Sounds like a tall order. And it is. Consensus, and the details of governance, usually evolve over time. Successful examples of communally managed commons are mostly found in small traditional societies, where local values and ways of caring for those things deemed most valuable have evolved over time, for instance among lobster fishermen in Maine, or on village-owned lands along the slopes of mountains in Japan, or along communally managed irrigation ditches in the highlands of New Mexico. But systems to manage a commons on the basis of fairness and sustainability can also be invented, worked out on the spot if the need is pressing enough, as with solutions to the grazing problems on public lands in the watersheds coming off the Whitehorse Mountains in southeastern Oregon, or the work done by the Byrne family to solve their problems on grazing lands along upstream Lost River watersheds west of Clear Lake Reservoir.

American white pelicans, Clear Lake, California.

Arriving at consensus means arriving at complete agreement. But that's a concept ordinarily interpreted as unworkable. Groups trying to define the public will usually consider wide public acceptance as consensus. Close enough. Total endorsement is an impossible goal.

When Senator Hatfield organized the Hatfield Working Group in 1994, he asked them to proceed as a consensus-decision-making organization. In 1996, when the United States Senate created the Upper Klamath Basin Working Group (formalizing the Hatfield group) as a pilot public advisory committee authorized to spend $1 million per year for five years so long as federal monies were matched by other funds, they were also organized as a consensus-decision-making group.

Consensus decision making, however, while giving the appearance of being democratic, is not for everyone. Wendell Wood said I'd been "talking to the compromisers." He meant the Upper Klamath Basin Working Group. The processes of consensus seem to often involve compromise. People ordinarily take a long time finding agreement on "dollar-and-lifestyle" issues and then come up with "lowest-common-denominator" solutions (which don't solve much but don't offend anybody). There's no substitute for talking and talking, meeting after meeting. It can get boring; participants sometimes agree to things they don't really believe in, just so they can go home (the trouble starts when they realize the implications of what they've agreed to). Or, they just quit the process and get on the telephone to their lawyer.

And the processes of consensus decision making can be easily manipulated. Appointed boards ordinarily represent the power brokers who appointed them. Consensus groups made up of local citizens called "stakeholders" are likely to represent local economic interests. And consensus groups can easily be as guilty of cronyism, under-the-table deal making, and secret agendas as any other group of citizens. Which doesn't make a strong case for trusting in the ability of entities like the Upper Klamath Basin Working Group to make objective decisions about the management of nationally owned properties like the wildlife refuges in the Klamath Basin.

It's the task of leadership, in democratically organized human activities, to provide the community with an open forum in which citizens can talk about courses of action. Having participated in the decision making, the leadership must respect and act out the decisions of the communal mind. It's a process that never stops. Actions have to be tried, evaluated, and rethought, over and over. And, always, onstage before the community. No hints of secret dealings or special privilege. People in the Klamath Basin must find a way to convince a national electorate that they are not being asked to endorse a set of done deals cooked up by a local economic elite.

The commons is community. Unfortunately, our mistakes, well-meant or actively malicious, our selfishness and our contrariness, our difficulties with governance, are also part of the commons. The process of consensus is, however—as the community tries to say what it wants, how it wants to function, what it cherishes and demands to see preserved—the best game in town.

The notion of water as tool and commodity, to be used rather than conserved, oftentimes best used outside the stream where it originates, was institutionalized in the West. Traditional western water law, according to Charles Wilkinson, Moses Lasky Professor of Law at the University of Colorado School of Law, who wrote the standard law-school texts on federal public land law and on Indian law, is dominated by "extreme deference to individual decisions to the exclusion of larger societal concerns; stable priority for historic uses; preferences for consumptive, usually commercial uses; a lack of protection for in-stream flows; and the provision of subsidized water for irrigators. Furthermore, the state laws made no place for Indian rights." Wilkinson also says, "All state constitutions or statutes declared water to be public, but nearly all water was appropriated in the form of vested property rights for private gain." The result, he says, was that "public resources were thrown open to virtually unfettered private exploitation." It was a policy designed to encourage settlement and growth of commerce. But the West is settled. Many westerners question the social price of continued economic growth as they see their land and water resources, which can be thought of as money in the public bank, being ruined.

In the year 2000 the population of the American West stands at around 60 million. Some 80 percent of those people live in cities like Denver, Phoenix, and Los Angeles. They want water, and tend to demand that wild ecologies be preserved. Western water-law priorities, responding to cultural evolution, seem sure to change. Some of the changes aren't going to be easy for many rural Westerners to accept. National and state lawmakers will be responding to demands that they recognize (1) that public interests take precedence over the rights of individuals, (2) that there is widespread concern over the health of our ecologies, (3) that there are objections to subsidized water projects, (4) that the public is aware of the economic value of natural beauties, (5) that the loss of farmlands and communities may occur when water rights are transferred to cities, and (6) that Indian rights are often senior and must be to some considerable degree fulfilled.

In particular, western courts are recognizing limits on private water rights, for example, observing (1) the state's right to regulate water in the interest of efficiency, (2) the fact that that water pollution law often conflicts with established uses, (3) the seniority of Indian rights, and (4) an absolute need to respond to the demands of the Endangered Species Act. No western water rights, it's clear, except those deemed to be in the public interest, will ever again be absolute. It's also clear that these are considerations that are likely to be of enormous consequence to water users in the Klamath Basin.

Oregon courts have decreed that it's time for water right adjudication in the Klamath Basin. Specific rights will be defined. Nobody, not the ranchers and farmers, not the wildlife refuge managers, not the tribes, is going to get all of what they claim. Established patterns will be reconsidered on the basis of wisest and best use, for all of society.

Value systems mutate and evolve. As Aldo Leopold told us a generation ago—tinker with one thing, and we alter the flow of everything. The changes being lived out in the Klamath Basin are part of these inexorable processes. Denial and anger won't get them stopped. Rage against change will in the long run be mainly useless.

Willows,
Lower Klamath Lake,
California.

"A land ethic, then, reflects the existence of an ecological conscience, and this in turn reflects a conviction of individual responsibility for the health of the land."

Citizens in the Klamath Basin have a choice. They can work together and resolve their common problems. Or someone in a courtroom, with other agendas, will call the shots. Leopold's definition of responsibilities is simple. He says we must never betray life. But establishing priorities, inventing techniques, is another matter. What's most important, a threatened species of fish or the irrigation rights of farmers along the Lost River? Leopold doesn't have any easy answers. There aren't going to be any. People in the Klamath Basin are stuck with working it out for themselves. Cultures learn to use technologies appropriate to the place where they live. Or, they wreck their homelands and vanish. Sounds melodramatic, but it's been historically true, over and over.

CONTINUITIES

Conservationists are interested in preserving life in its necessary multiplicity. All the species, every one. And in promoting thriving human neighborhoods. Nobody advocates destroying life or communities.

On spring mornings when I was a child in Warner I would stand out in early morning under a clean spring sky and listen to the sighing of wings and ducks and geese calling as vast flocks flew north on their way to nesting grounds on the tundra. Everything I loved was nearby.

Consequently, I attach great importance to the preservation of such birds and their flyway, where they live. That attachment, as I age, is increasingly close to central in my life. I am willing to devote energies, and even occasional bits of money, to ensure the well-being of waterbirds. I'll vote for politicians who seem determined to work on behalf of preserving birds. I respond to what's called the aesthetic or spiritual argument in favor of environmental preservation.

There's also a practical argument. It's thought by many that the most important thing happening on earth is what's called the gene-pool crisis. We are participating in a disaster, an eco-catastrophe—devastation of the interwoven system of life on our planet. Today, it's said, is the most critical period in the 3.5-billion-year history of life on earth. By 2050 half the species alive today may be extinct. Two-thirds of the bird species are endangered; one in ten faces extinction. Fifty plant species become extinct every day. Deep-sea fisheries vanish as we watch (for instance, Klamath River salmon). The litany goes on. Our earth is suffering deforestation, desertification, acid rain, radioactive fallout, chemical contamination, and consequent ozone-layer and climate disturbances. Biological interactions necessary to sus-

Black-crowned night heron,
Upper Klamath Lake,
Oregon.

tain and ensure the continuities of life on the planet are astonishingly complex. As the gene pool shrinks, so do possibilities. Alter the gene pool enough, and the quickness of life itself will be utterly transmogrified.

Care for our physical heritage is a fundamental responsibility, of our species, to our species. It is our duty to preserve biodiversity. Biologist Edward O. Wilson has said the loss of genetic diversity is "the folly our descendants are least likely to forgive us." That thought rings in the emotional life of people everywhere, and in the economic life of the Klamath Basin.

Then there's the psychic crisis. Humans evolved on savannas in Africa, in the midst of thronging life. As species vanish, our children are sentenced to increasingly solitary kinds of confinement. Possibilities for connection disappear. People become increasingly isolated, disconnected, and disoriented. We are the dominant creatures on earth. We exist at the top of the power chain. We get to call the shots. But as we increasingly isolate ourselves, we find life closer and closer to spiritually unlivable. We see evidence of that fact in our news-

Eileen and Bob McKay,
third-generation cattle
ranchers, Lower Klamath
Lake, California, 1998.

papers every day—anger, madness, bombings. We see people ruined by despair, talking to themselves. We look away. There is nothing, we think, to be done. But there is.

Efforts to protect waterbirds are efforts to protect the specifically sacred, by which I mean life. The weeding and poisoning are ways of courting craziness. That's the existential half of the practical line.

Preserving ecologies is only half an agenda for a sustainable future. The other half swings on the survival of villages, human-scaled communities like those formed by ranchers who live around Fort Klamath, or farmers in towns like Merrill or Tulelake (or in city neighborhoods or on college campuses or in military encampments or, maybe, in e-mail collectives). Villages are an essential part of the environment our species has evolved within; they are part of our native habitat, the only kind of place where most of us can live in psychic comfort.

Citizens working to preserve both the environment and communities are part of a world political constituency that is growing very rapidly. The yearning to preserve both waterbirds and small towns is commonplace and well regarded. It is driven by an utterly natural, built-into-the-genes urge to care for our species. It is unavoidably influencing every effort to consider values in the Klamath Basin.

On a bright fall day Tupper took me out to visit Bob and Eileen McKay at their ranch south of Otey Island. Bob broke off welding and took us into the house for coffee and talk about

Ross' geese,
Tule Lake, California.

his family (they've been in the basin for three generations) and the ways livestock and waterbirds coexist.

"Some of the best spring feed those birds get," Bob said, "comes off our meadows. Ask those fellows at the refuge. In the twenties, before they had canals, when the alkali ground blew, we fed cows on the blow ground and tied it down. The cows tromped in manure and feed and built up the soil. We learned to fence the cows off ditch banks. Fields won't go back to nature. Nobody even knows what nature is. The Indians were working this place a long time before we came along."

A mile or so away, on Sheepy Creek, archeologists have found three villages, one on top of the other, the oldest dating back some twelve thousand years, at a site called Night-Fire Island. I'm reminded that we define ourselves by telling stories, and that telling stories around the night fire was a human beginning.

Those ancient people acted out lives that in essence were not much different from ours. We dig up charred bone and obsidian points; we try to imagine their days. It's my guess they climbed Otey Butte in the autumn twilight and thrilled to the look of flying birds.

Maybe, if Klamath people are lucky, citizens willing to give their energies away like gifts, for the well-being of their common society, will turn out to be generous and tough enough to work through the maze of problems and come out on the other side inhabiting the happy land that's so clearly there.

Eileen McKay trains sheepdogs. As we left her, in sunset light, penning her sheep for the night, with her dogs, carrying a crook, Eileen looked like someone to be envied, immersed in our endless task.

INDEX

Page references in italics refer to photographs.

Adams, J. Frank, 52
Agency Lake, Oregon: agriculture in, 130; Native American preconquest territory, 37
Agency Lake Ranch, 140–141
Ager's Cafe, 83
agribusiness, 86–87; Native American water rights and, 93; organic research by, 104; restoration and, 139
agriculture: alkaline soils and, 77, 78–79; conflict with Native Americans and, 41, 93–95; economic fading of, 102, 104; grazing (*see* grazing); irrigation (*see* irrigation); labor of, 86, 105; on lease lands (*see* lease-land program); mechanization of, 86–87; organic (*see* organic farming); pesticides (*see* pesticides); preservation of lands, 12; species endangerment and (*see under* species endangerment); transition to organic, 104, 125–126, 128, 131, 132–133; water rights and, 91, 93; wildlife refuges in conflict with, 77–79, 85–86; yields, 52. *See also* environmentalists; potato farming; ranching and ranches
alcohol, Native American deaths and, 49

algae: as agricultural product, 104; oxygen depletion by, 135, 141
alkalinity, 77, 78–79, 149
American avocet, *143*
American marten, *70*
American white pelicans, 75, *75*, *159*
animism, 35–36
Ankeny-Henley Canal, Oregon, 51
Aqua Glass, 102
Ardoin, Allen, 127
Aristotle, 157
Aspen Lake, Oregon, 150–151
Associated Press, 127
Associated Sportsmen of California, 85
Audubon Society, 73, 74, 79, 99
Austrians, 55

badgers, *63*
balancing water, 4
bald eagles, *124*, *125*, *138*
Bare Island, Oregon, *92*
Barrett, Glenn, 91, *91*
Barrett, Linda, *91*
Barrett, Michael, *91*
Basey, Clinton, 24, *25*, 147
Beatty, Oregon, *107*
Bend, Oregon, 103, 104
Biological Survey, U.S., 79
biomass, 127

biotic community, 6–7
birds: desire to protect, as self-care, 163, 165; hunting (*see* hunting); populations, 1, 29, 74–75, 79, 147, 149. *See also* wildlife refuges; *names of individual species*
Bitney, Raymond, 48
black-crowned night heron, *164*
Black Jim, 46
blacktailed jackrabbit, *64*
bobcat, *95*
Bogus Creek, *96*
Bohlman, Herman, 73, 74
Bonneville Dam, 97
Boston Charlie, 46
botulism, 79, 85, 150
Boundary Canyon, 150–151
Brennan, Barry, *113*
Brower, David, 97
Bryant Mountain, Oregon, *154*
buckaroos. *See* cowboys
buffalo, 4
bull trout, 15, *15*
bureaucracy: advocacy for local community, 159–160; gridlock of, 98–100; vs. local needs, 19–20, 21, 98–100; Westerners and, 18–19. *See also* democracy
Bureau of Indian Affairs, 48, 99
Bureau of Land Management, 21, 137, 139

The authors at Marsh Island
Ranch, Lower Klamath Lake,
California, 1998.

WILLIAM KITTREDGE (*left*) grew up on the MC Ranch in southeastern Oregon, farmed until he was thirty-five, studied in the Writers' Workshop at the University of Iowa, and was Regents Professor of English and Creative Writing at the University of Montana when he retired in 1997.

Kittredge has held a Stegner Fellowship at Stanford (1973–74), received two Writing Fellowships from the National Endowment for the Arts (1974, 1982) and two Pacific Northwest Bookseller Awards for Excellence (1984, 1987), won the Montana Governor's Award for the Arts (1986), and was a co-winner of the Montana Committee for the Humanities Award for Humanist of the Year (1989). In 1994 he was co-winner of the National Endowment for the Humanities' Charles Frankel Prize for service to the humanities.

Kittredge has published in *Atlantic, Harper's, Esquire, Time, Newsweek, TriQuarterly, Outside,* and the *Paris Review.* He has co-authored nine novels in the Cord series of westerns (Ballantine Books) and published two collections of short fiction, *The Van Gogh Field and Other Stories* (University of Missouri Press, 1979) and *We Are Not in This Together* (Graywolf, 1984), as well as a book of essays, *Owning It All* (Graywolf, 1987). He was co-editor of *The Last Best Place: A Montana Anthology,* co-winner of the Neil Simon Award from American Playhouse for his work on *Heartland,* and co-producer of *A River Runs Through It.* His book-length memoir, *Hole in the Sky,* was published by Knopf in 1992 and Vintage in 1993. A book of essays, *Who Owns the West?* came out from Mercury House in 1996, and *The Portable Western Reader* was published by Viking/Penguin in 1997.

TUPPER ANSEL BLAKE (*right*) divides his time among his professional wildlife photography, his commitment to bringing conservation issues before the public, and his restoration of wetlands with his wife, Madeleine, at their ranch in the Klamath Basin. His work has been published in *Audubon, Defenders of Wildlife, Ducks Unlimited, Harper's, Life, National Geographic, National Wildlife, Natural History, Nature Conservancy, Newsweek, Pacific Discovery, Sierra, Smithsonian, Sports Illustrated,* and *Wilderness.* His three previous books are *Wild California: Vanishing Lands, Vanishing Wildlife* (with A. Starker Leopold, 1985), *Tracks in the Sky: Wildlife and Wetlands of the Pacific Flyway* (with Peter Steinhart, 1987), and *Two Eagles/Dos Águilas: The Natural World of the United States–Mexico Borderlands* (with Peter Steinhart, 1994).

Exhibitions of his work have hung at the Santa Barbara Museum of Natural History; Oregon Historical Society; Utah Museum of Natural History; Chicago Academy of Sciences; Thunder Bay Art Gallery (Thunder Bay, Ontario); Royal British Columbia Museum; Alaska State Museum; IBM Headquarters (Suffern, New York); National Museum of Natural History, Smithsonian Institution; Dallas Museum of Natural History; California Academy of Sciences; Pacific Science Center (Seattle, Washington); San Diego Natural History Museum; United Nations (New York City); Fernbank Museum of Natural History (Atlanta, Georgia); New Mexico Museum of Natural History; and Witte Museum (San Antonio, Texas).

He received the 1983 Ansel Adams Photography Award of the Sierra Club; the 1986 California Nature Conservancy Service Award; the 1988 Distinguished Alumni Award, University of California at Santa Barbara; and the 1995 Silver Medal for Notable Contribution to Publishing, the Commonwealth Club of California.

MADELEINE GRAHAM BLAKE (*center*), a native of Klamath Falls, Oregon, is a photographer, exhibition designer, and graphic artist. Studying photography as a fine art medium at San Francisco State College, she won the Condé Naste College Competition for photography in 1970. Her work has hung in museums and galleries throughout California, including the Pasadena Museum of Art, Monterey Museum of Art, and Friends of Photography gallery in Carmel. Reproductions of her imagery have been included in numerous publications.

An exhibition designer at the California Academy of Sciences, she created major exhibits for such notable artists as Ansel Adams, Imogen Cunningham, Robert Bateman, Roger Tory Petersen, Andy Warhol, Maynard Dixon, Galen Rowell, Tupper Ansel Blake, and Gary Larson. Leaving the Academy in 1988, she established her own business, producing exhibitions for which she is the primary graphic designer. Her client list includes the Smithsonian Institution, Wells Fargo Foundation, Bank of America, Arthur Anderson Company, Commonwealth of the Mariana Islands, California Forest Products Commission, Marin Agricultural Land Trust, and Guide Dogs for the Blind.

She currently divides her time between a home and design office in Marin County and her darkroom and art studio at Marsh Island Ranch in the Klamath Basin.

MICK is a Jack Russell terrier with an extra dose of beagle. He retrieves ducks, flushes quail, eats Rocky Mountain oysters at spring brandings, and generally follows the trail of good times.

Text:	12/15 Bembo
Display:	Onyx & Bembo
Design:	Steve Renick
Composition:	Integrated Composition Systems
Printing and binding:	C & C Offset Printing Co., Ltd